DRUG ABUSE AND DRUG COUNSELING

DRUG ABUSE AND DRUG COUNSELING

A CASE APPROACH

THOMAS WEISMAN
Case Western Reserve University

ADVISORY EDITOR
ALBERT SATTIN, M.D.
Departments of Pharmacology and Psychiatry
School of Medicine
Case Western Reserve University

CONSULTING EDITOR
WILLIAM T. STICKLEY, PH.D.
Director
Health Sciences Communications Center
Case Western Reserve University

THE PRESS OF
CASE WESTERN RESERVE UNIVERSITY
Cleveland and London/1972

This publication was supported in part by NIH grant LM 00673 from the National Library of Medicine.

To my parents and to Alan

CONTENTS

PREFACE

This book attempts to provide a foundation of pharmacological knowledge upon which the reader, using counseling abilities developed in other areas, can build confidence and skill in counseling those with drug-related problems. Such counseling is in many ways similar to that for other problems. Our intention is that, having read this book, you will feel more confident in dealing with people whose problems may involve some form of drug abuse.

Each of the seven chapters in the book deals with a single group of psychoactive drugs and consists of a short expository section, a true-false question-and-answer section, and a set of case problems. The expository sections contain a "core" of information in as concise a form as possible. This is essential information, which must be understood. The true-false questions are of two kinds: review questions and questions which state some common "folk beliefs" about the drugs in question. Although many of these questions cannot be answered correctly using only the information presented in the expository sections, their purpose is neither to trick nor frustrate the reader. Rather, the answers following the questions are designed to introduce new information in a fashion which promotes effective learning. Because this new information is associated with specific questions which have been raised in the reader's mind, it is more likely to be retained.

Chapter 1, "The Narcotic Analgesics," contains discussions of terms generally applicable to drug abuse of all kinds.

Finally, each chapter closes with a set of case problems. These case problems confront the reader with a realistic counseling situation and require him to choose one of several possible alternatives. Each alternative is then discussed with regard to its appropriateness in the given situation. Some of the alternatives offered may seem trivial or even silly; however, they are presented in order to elucidate an important point in the discussion which follows each case. For this reason, it is important to read the case discussions in their entirety—it is often just as important to know why one alternative is *not* appropriate as it is to know why another one is most appropriate. Each course of action must be considered in the context of the specific case involved and the only general rule which can be uniformly applied is *primum non nocere*—above all, do not cause any harm.

ACKNOWLEDGMENTS

I would like to express my gratitude to the many people without whose generous efforts this book would never have come to fruition. Dr. John L. Caughey, Jr. was responsible for my coming to Case Western Reserve University. He has always been willing and ready to give me sound advice and guidance whenever I needed it. Dr. T. Hale Ham, director of the Division of Research in Medical Education, committed himself to support my work at its very inception, as did Dr. William T. Stickley. Without their faith and encouragement, this book would have been just another unrealized idea. Dr. Stickley also assisted with the format of the book, which is adapted from earlier work done by Dr. Morton A. Stenchever and Dr. Stickley. The entire faculty and staff of the Division of Research in Medical Education gave of their time and effort to help test the manuscript through all of its various revisions. Special thanks go to Dr. Marcia Z. Wile, Catherine L. Ullman, and Carolyn R. Kraynak of the Division. Miss Kraynak cheerfully typed the bulk of the manuscript as many times as was necessary and helped in countless other ways. Thanks go also to Mary Lou Cantini who contributed some very important typing on short notice.

There is no room to list all of the students, faculty, physicians, and other professionals who reviewed the manuscript and who helped in so many other ways. Any success of this book as a teaching device is due in large part to the constructive suggestions of these unsung heroes.

The staff of the Press of Case Western Reserve University have been most helpful in the development of the book,

xii   DRUG ABUSE AND DRUG COUNSELING

through their faith in a young author, and by providing encouragement when it was most needed. They taught me a great deal about writing and publishing while coaxing the manuscript through its evolution. Mary Lou Conlin was largely responsible for the transition of the manuscript from a draft to final copy. I learned more about prose writing from her than from any other English teacher or professor.

I wish to thank the Free Clinic of Cleveland for the opportunity of working with people who had drug-related problems. Much of what follows is based on what I learned in my work at the Free Clinic.

Although we have never met, I must express my gratitude to Dr. Jerome H. Jaffe. His chapters in Goodman and Gilman's *The Pharmacological Basis of Therapeutics* were responsible for my becoming interested in the area of drug abuse, and many of the paths followed in this book were originally charted by Dr. Jaffe.

Dr. Albert Sattin has contributed more to this book than any other single person. His breadth of knowledge of neuropharmacology is matched only by the acuity of his psychiatric insights. Dr. Sattin and I have worked together for nearly three years. During this time my respect for him has never stopped growing.

Finally, I want to thank my wife Lorraine for putting up with me while this book was being written. Her substantive assistance, understanding, and confidence saw me through long nights and trying days of writing and revising. My gratitude for her ideas, kind words, and gentle encouragement can never be adequately expressed.

Thomas Weisman

DRUG ABUSE AND DRUG COUNSELING

Chapter 1

THE NARCOTIC ANALGESICS

A twenty-two year-old man comes to see you for "personal problems." He is a stocky, handsome, healthy-looking fellow who appears distraught and close to tears. When you ask him what is troubling him, he says that most of the time he feels like killing himself.

He has been addicted to heroin for six months, he reports, and wants desperately to quit using it, but he doesn't know how. He doesn't really know how it happened, he says, but he got in with the wrong group of friends and started using heroin. He says that he knows he was stupid for doing it and that he wants to quit more than anything else in the world.

When you ask him to tell you some more about himself, he replies that he was in the Marine Corps after high school and that he drank a lot but had no drug problems then. He now has a job in construction, and he lives at home with his parents. At this point, he starts crying and says his parents are wonderful people who would just die if they found out about his drug use. His girl knows, he says, and has been very understanding and willing to help him. So far, he has been able to hold his job and hide his addiction from his parents and most of his friends, but he doesn't know how much longer he can go on as he has been and doesn't know how he can stop using heroin.

In this situation, how would you counsel the young man?

TERMS RELATING TO DRUG ABUSE

In order to help a person whose problems relate to the use of some drug that affects his thinking, feeling, or behavior, a counselor—whether he is a physician, a social worker, an educator or a parent—should know about such drugs and their effects and should also be familiar with the meaning of several terms that are commonly used in connection with drug abuse: *addiction, physical dependence, withdrawal, withdrawal syndrome, psychological dependence, drug dependence,* and *tolerance.* There are no universally agreed upon definitions for some of these terms, but the definitions given below have widespread acceptance. Throughout this book, the use of these terms will be consistent with these definitions; the word *addiction,* for example, will have the same meaning whenever used.

Addiction is a behavior pattern of compulsive drug use, characterized by an overwhelming preoccupation with the use of the drug and securing its continual supply and by a high tendency to relapse after withdrawal.[1] Note that this definition describes a behavior pattern rather than any specific pharmacological interaction. Furthermore, it is often not possible to precisely identify the point at which compulsive drug use becomes addiction.

Physical dependence, on the other hand, can be measured with somewhat more precision. When a drug user has developed physical dependence, *withdrawal,* which is the cessation of drug use, will produce a characteristic set of physical symptoms that are specific for each group of drugs that produces physical dependence. Such a set of symptoms is called a *withdrawal syndrome.* The more abrupt the withdrawal, the severer the syndrome. The term "withdrawal syndrome" refers to no psychological reaction, but rather to a physical reaction; in the absence of a withdrawal syndrome, there is no physical dependence, and vice-versa. It is entirely possible, in this conceptual framework, to be addicted to a drug without being physically dependent, or physically dependent on a drug without being addicted to it.

Psychological dependence is the condition that exists when the effects produced by a drug have become necessary to the individual in order to maintain an optimal state of well-being. The intensity of psychological dependence may range from mild desire to a craving, and this dependence may lead to the behavior pattern characterized as addiction.

The patterns of drug use can be considered as a continuum, with total abstinence at one extreme and addiction at the other, and with experimental use and social use somewhere in between total abstinence and addiction. *Drug dependence* is characterized by a pattern of drug use that we may be reluctant to call addiction but that involves a moderately high degree of psychological dependence and compulsive use.

Tolerance is a physical phenomenon that develops in chronic users of certain drugs. When an individual develops tolerance to a drug, repeated equal doses of the drug have less and less effect and steadily increasing doses are required to attain the same effect.

NARCOTIC ANALGESICS

The young man in the above case had a problem with heroin. Heroin belongs to a group of drugs called the narcotic analgesics. An analgesic is an agent which produces insensibility to pain without loss of consciousness (aspirin is a commonly-used analgesic). The narcotic analgesics are the drugs whose effects resemble those of morphine, an opiate alkaloid, in yielding a very pronounced analgesia. Their other effects include drowsiness, respiratory depression, cough suppression, nausea, vomiting, constipation, and miosis (pinpoint pupils). Other drugs besides morphine in this class are codeine, another opiate alkaloid; heroin, a derivative of morphine; meperidine (Demerol) and methadone, a synthetic morphine substitute.

The chief chemical use of the narcotic analgesics is for the relief of severe pain, and for this they are unsurpassed. Pain is thought to consist of two components, a purely sensory component and a reactive component. Under conditions of extreme psychological stress, such as on a battlefield, people have been known to tolerate the pain of grave injuries (the reactive component is ignored), even though their capacity to receive sensation (the sensory component) is relatively unaltered. The narcotic analgesics seem to delete the reactive component of pain—the suffering—without affecting the actual sensation. Patients often report that they can still *feel* the pain, but that it doesn't *hurt* them.

The chief medical indication for the use of these agents is pain, either acute or chronic. However, pain is often a vital diagnostic sign. Usually, narcotic analgesics are not administered by a physician until a diagnosis is made. One exception to this practice would be a case where the patient's pain is so disabling as to seriously interfere with the physician's ability to obtain the patient's history or to make a physical examination.

Features common to all of the narcotic analgesics are the development of tolerance and physical dependence with continued use. Furthermore, addiction to any of these agents is possible; however, this does not invariably occur. The withdrawal syndrome characteristic of the narcotic analgesics includes the following symptoms: dilated pupils, sneezing, runny nose, anxiety, restlessness, tremors, diarrhea, cramps, vomiting, chills and flushing, pain in muscles and bone, and waves of gooseflesh. The symptoms begin between four to six hours after the last dose of heroin or morphine and reach their peak in twenty-four to seventy-two hours. The withdrawal symptoms usually last no longer than five to seven days. Drugs that are excreted more slowly, such as methadone, produce a milder withdrawal syndrome, which may last ten to fourteen days. Because of the gastrointestinal symptoms (vomiting and diarrhea), it is possible for a patient to become dehydrated and even to suffer peripheral vascular collapse (acute loss of blood pressure) if neglected. Death, however, is a rare event.

Although all of the narcotic analgesics have similar effects, heroin has become the chief member of this group to be abused. This is due largely to its being both highly potent by weight and very easy and cheap to manufacture from morphine. Although heroin could have the same medical use as morphine or meperidine, all possession of heroin has been made illegal. Thus, there is no medical supply of this drug that might serve as a source for diversion to addicts.

Heroin can be administered orally (very rare), by inhalation ("snorting," "sniffing"), subcutaneous injection ("popping," "skin grafting"), or by intravenous injection ("mainlining"). Intravenous injection is usually the method preferred by addicts and gives the quickest and most pronounced drug effect (a "rush" or thrill), which is described as a warm flushing of the skin and a feeling like an orgasm. The addict then drifts off into a euphoric state; that is, he has a feeling of well-being without any objective reasons for such a feeling. The drug effect lasts three to five hours. Because of the illegality of the drug, the supply is usually controlled by criminal organizations. Since the addict needs increasingly larger amounts because of drug tolerance, it is not unusual for him to spend as much as $100 a day and more for heroin. Many addicts resort to theft or prostitution to raise the money to support their habit.[2]

There is no legal barrier to the use of commercially available narcotic analgesics in medical practice for:

1. administration to patients with acute pain;
2. administration to patients with intractable pain;
3. administration to aged and debilitated patients with drug dependence on the morphine-type analgesics, where withdrawal is potentially lethal;
4. administration to drug-dependent and formerly drug-dependent patients with other medical problems.

It is legal to administer narcotic analgesics to an addict to relieve acute withdrawal symptoms or as interim medication while the addict is on a waiting list for admission to a treatment facility. It is also legal to administer morphine-like drugs, combined with other treatment, preparatory to withdrawal. Continued administration of drugs solely for the maintenance of dependence is not legal, except in a special situation. Such a situation is the methadone maintenance or (methadone "blockade") treatment for narcotic addicts. This treatment has been increasingly applied since its initial development in the early 1960's.

Methadone is a synthetic narcotic analgesic with some very important properties. First, it is highly effective, whether administered orally or parenterally (by injection). Second, methadone accumulates in the body, if administered over a period of time. Tolerance develops as the drug accumulates.

When the drug intake is abruptly stopped, withdrawal symptoms do not appear until more than twenty-four hours after the last dose, and the symptoms are less severe than those associated with other narcotics. In contrast, a person who is physically dependent on other narcotics would begin to experience withdrawal symptoms more acutely and more severely within four to six hours after his last dose of the drug.

Methadone maintenance (or methadone blockade) takes advantage of the special properties of this drug. Addicts are given methadone orally (usually dissolved in fruit juice) in amounts sufficient to block their withdrawal symptoms. As tolerance develops, the dose is gradually raised to quite high levels. Because of the oral route of administration, there is no "rush" (as compared to intravenous use); because of the tolerance that develops, little or no euphoria ("high") or disabling somnolence (sleepiness) is experienced by the addict; and because of the persistence of the drug in the body, only one dose per day is necessary to prevent withdrawal symptoms.

The advantages of this program are that the methadone seems to block the addict's compulsive craving for narcotics (whether heroin or other narcotics including methadone itself); it removes the economic necessity of raising the $50 to $100 a day to subsidize the addiction, since methadone is cheaper than the fruit juice it is dissolved in; its presence in the body blocks the effects of an injection of heroin and thereby removes the component of euphoria from the spectrum of the addiction; and finally, when combined with a program of support and counseling, it seems to work on many addicts who have failed at other methods of rehabilitation. Furthermore, it works on an outpatient basis. The main disadvantage of methadone maintenance is that it maintains a physical dependence indefinitely. But experience accumulated through many maintenance programs indicates that patients no longer manifest the behavior patterns of addiction. They no longer have an overwhelming preoccupation with the use of heroin (or methadone), and there has been little tendency toward relapse in the well-run programs. Patients tend to become employed, to stabilize family relationships, and to become productive members of society. In effect, they lose their addiction, though they retain their physical dependence on narcotic analgesics.[3]

Methadone is also used to withdraw addicts. Addicts are given methadone orally in amounts sufficient to block their withdrawal symptoms and are maintained on this dose for several days. Then they are either tapered gradually from this dose or abruptly withdrawn. In either case, because of the persistence of methadone in the body, withdrawal symptoms from this drug are reduced in severity but last somewhat longer. Thus, methadone withdrawal is a way to ease the physical discomfort of the addict during the withdrawal period. Methadone withdrawal is most successful in a controlled setting, such as a hospital, but has been used with some success on an outpatient basis.

A therapeutic approach currently being investigated is narcotic antagonist maintenance. Narcotic antagonists are substances that are chemically related to the narcotic analgesics but that almost completely block most of their effects. Blockade by narcotic antagonists prevents both the narcotic effects and tolerance to narcotics. (In contrast, tolerance to the narcotic in methadone "blockade" is already so great that the effect of additional narcotic is barely felt. The pharmacological difference between the two types of blockade relates to the presence or absence of tolerance to the narcotic.) The narcotic antagonists are useful in the treatment of narcotic overdose, will block the effects of a later dose of narcotics, and will precipitate immediate withdrawal symptoms in a physically dependent person. In these programs, antagonists are administered to patients on a daily basis. The antagonists prevent them from experiencing any drug effect, no matter how much narcotic they may inject.

Another approach to the treatment of narcotic addiction is through the therapeutic community. Synanon, Phoenix House, and Odyssey House are examples of such communities. The "rules" of the community may require a member's "cold turkey" withdrawal (abrupt cessation with no tapering or pharmacological replacement), and the leaders rely upon peer pressure, a sense of belonging, and shared experiences as the means for making the addict develop and sustain a drug-free pattern of living. The members of a community attempt to substitute closeness and shared feelings for drug use. This approach has been successful for certain groups of addicts, particularly those in their teens. But the success of a community depends a great deal upon the skill of its leaders and upon the unwavering motivation and commitment of its participants.

QUESTIONS

The following section contains a set of true-false questions related to narcotic analgesics. Such a true-false section is found in each chapter of this workbook. Some of the questions review material presented in the expository section, and some present new material, but in the context of exploring common myths and "folk beliefs." Each set of questions is followed by a discussion of each answer.

1. The majority of normal, pain-free individuals find the effects of opiates quite unpleasant.

<u>True</u> or false? ......

2. Babies born to women who are physically dependent on narcotic analgesics are themselves physically dependent on narcotic analgesics.

<u>True</u> or false? ......

3. The "pusher" plays a major role in enticing non-users to the use of narcotic analgesics.

True or <u>false</u>? ......

4. Everyone has the same chance of becoming a narcotic analgesic addict when exposed to the drug.

True or <u>false</u>? ......

5. Narcotic analgesics enhance the sexual drive in an addict.

True or <u>false</u>? ......

6. Narcotic analgesics in themselves cause direct physiologi-

cal damage with prolonged use.

                                    True or false? . . . . . .

7. Morphine will relieve the withdrawal symptoms of a person who is physically dependent on heroin.

                                    True or false? . . . . . .

8. The withdrawal syndrome of narcotic analgesics is very frequently fatal.

                                    True or false? . . . . . .

9. The chief cause of death in narcotic analgesic overdose is cardiac failure.

                                    True or false? . . . . . .

10. The abuse potential of some of the narcotic analgesics is significantly less than the abuse potential of heroin.

                                    True or false? . . . . . .

11. It would be possible to use heroin or morphine instead of methadone in a long-term maintenance program.

                                    True or false? . . . . . .

12. Heroin has no therapeutic usefulness.

                                    True or false? . . . . . .

13. Self-administration of the narcotic analgesics is the preferred method for patients in pain.

                                    True or false? . . . . . .

14. Occasional use of heroin does not necessarily lead to addiction.

                                    True or false? . . . . . .

ANSWERS

1. The majority of normal, pain-free individuals find the effects of opiates quite unpleasant.

Answer: *True*. Furthermore, many addicts often recall that their first experiences with narcotics were unpleasant. There is a learning process where the addict learns to perceive euphoria (a sense of well-being) despite nausea and dizziness. When these drugs are given to patients in pain, euphoria is frequent; but, when they are given to patients not in pain, dysphoria (an unpleasant feeling, the opposite of euphoria) is frequent.

2. Babies born to women who are physically dependent on narcotic analgesics are themselves physically dependent on narcotic analgesics.

Answer: *True*. This is very important to know, for the withdrawal syndrome is very dangerous for a newborn and has to be handled with the utmost care. This is an example of physical dependence without addiction.

3. The "pusher" plays a major role in enticing non-users to the use of narcotic analgesics.

Answer: *False*. Most are introduced to the drug by other users, often their "friends." The pusher does not have to seek new users. It is a seller's market, and the risk is high. The pusher feels more comfortable when he deals with established addicts whom he knows he can trust. Usually, the demand for drugs is greater than the supply.[4]

4. Everyone has the same chance of becoming a narcotic analgesic addict when exposed to the drug.

14

Answer: *False*. People demonstrate tremendous differences in their ability to live without these drugs after having been exposed to them. Often, personality disturbances antedate the use of the drug. Usually only people who are suffering find the narcotic analgesics in any way pleasant. A study of schizophrenic patients, in whom severe physical dependence on narcotic analgesics had been induced, revealed that these patients could go through a complete withdrawal syndrome and exhibit no interest whatsoever in continuing the drug, even when it was demonstrated to them that repeated doses of the drug would relieve their withdrawal symptoms.[5] This study demonstrates that physical dependence does not always lead to addiction or even to psychological dependence.

5. Narcotic analgesics enhance the sexual drive in an addict.

Answer: *False*. The narcotic analgesics reduce all drives: the hunger drive, the pain drive, the aggression drives, and the sex drive. It is the addict's need for the drug rather than the effects of the drug that motivates such illegal activities as prostitution and thievery.

6. Narcotic analgesics in themselves cause direct physiological damage with prolonged use.

Answer: *False*. The narcotic analgesics by themselves cause no direct physiological damage, even with prolonged use. However, the death rate among addicts is several times higher than the death rate among comparable non-addict populations. The leading causes of death among addicts are overdosage, serum hepatitis and bacterial endocarditis through needle contamination, and suicide.[6] The possibility that chronic use of heroin or morphine produces genetic damage has not been adequately investigated.[7]

7. Morphine will relieve the withdrawal symptoms of a person who is physically dependent on heroin.

Answer: *True*. This phenomenon is called cross-dependence. Any of the narcotic analgesics will either partially or completely relieve the withdrawal symptoms of any other narcotic analgesic. However, the person still remains physically dependent; and as soon as the effect of the last dose wears off, the withdrawal symptoms begin again. The person is, in effect, physically dependent upon the whole class of narcotic analgesics, regardless of which particular drug it is that he is taking at the time.

8. The withdrawal syndrome of narcotic analgesics is very frequently fatal.

Answer: *False*. The withdrawal syndrome has been likened in severity to a bad case of influenza. It should be kept in mind, however, that some people, especially those who are elderly, debilitated, or malnourished, can die of influenza. This is also true of the withdrawal syndrome. Just because a withdrawal syndrome is not lethal does not mean that it is not unpleasant, as anyone who has tried to quit smoking cigarettes can easily testify.

9. The chief cause of death in narcotic analgesic overdose is cardiac failure.

Answer: *False*. The chief cause of death in overdose is anoxia (lack of oxygen). The narcotic analgesics reduce the responsiveness of the brain stem respiratory centers to carbon dioxide. The resultant slowing or even cessation of breathing causes the brain to die from lack of oxygen.[8] Another theory postulates that some addicts die of a massive allergic reaction to some contaminant or adulterant present in the drug. Although some evidence is consistent with this hypothesis, it has not yet been conclusively proven or disproven.[9]

10. The abuse potential (potential for addiction) of some of the narcotic analgesics is significantly less than the abuse potential of heroin.

Answer: *False*. There is no evidence at the present time that the abuse potential of any of the narcotic analgesics is *significantly* less than that of the others.

11. It would be possible to use heroin or morphine instead of methadone in a long-term maintenance program.

Answer: *True*. In fact, Great Britain has been experimenting with heroin maintenance programs. However, the use of methadone in maintenance programs has several advantages over the use of heroin or morphine. The two most important advantages are: methadone can be administered *orally,* thus obviating the needle habit; and methadone can be administered only once a day, but heroin or morphine must be administered every four to six hours to prevent the occurrence of withdrawal symptoms. As a result, a patient in a methadone maintenance program experiences neither the "rush" from the intravenous injection nor the cycle of "highs" and "lows" characteristic of the use of heroin or morphine. Consequently, daily functioning is less impaired by methadone than by heroin or morphine.

12. Heroin has no therapeutic usefulness.

Answer: *False*. Heroin was originally developed as a painkiller to replace morphine. The developers thought that it had a lower abuse potential than morphine. This is not true. The reason heroin is marketed illegally rather than morphine is that heroin is two to three times more potent *by weight*. This means that the effects of one pound of heroin compare to the effects of three pounds of morphine, and one pound of heroin is much easier to smuggle and market than three pounds of morphine.

13. Self-administration of the narcotic analgesics is the preferred method for patients in pain.

Answer: *False*. It is the self-administration of drugs and the consequent self-induced changes in mood that are most dangerous and that markedly raise the addiction liability of these drugs. This should be kept in mind by physicians, not only when treating patients but when they are tempted to treat themselves.

14. Occasional use of heroin does not necessarily lead to addiction.

Answer: *True*. Intermittent use of heroin in any fashion does not *necessarily* lead to addiction. Some persons will not become addicted, no matter how they try it. There is no way to predict, however, whether one will become a heroin addict before he does; then it is often too late. The risk of heroin addiction increases markedly with intravenous administration, but whether a person will or will not become addicted depends more on the individual than on the original route of administration. Those who will become addicts will almost always eventually use heroin intravenously, regardless of how they begin.

TREATMENT OF THE FIRST CASE

You should now be able to make logical decisions about counseling the young man whose problem was presented at the beginning of this chapter. Which of the following would you do?

    (A) Tell him that there is nothing you can do for him.
    (B) Tell him that he should have thought of the consequences before he became addicted.
    (C) Involve him in a methadone maintenance program.
    (D) Involve him in a methadone withdrawal program.
    (E) Report him to the police.
    (F) Refer him to a therapeutic community.
    (G) Suggest the following (write your own solution):

. . . .

. . . .

. . . .

. . . .

On the following pages, you will find a discussion of each of the solutions given above.

DISCUSSION

Telling the young heroin user that there is nothing you can do for him (A) is an abdication of professional responsibility. No matter how ill-equipped you are to deal with an addiction, you should always have the ability to give some comfort and reassurance to those who seek your aid. Even if you are not in a position to materially contribute to this young man's rehabilitation, you can help by referring him to those who are in a position to aid him. You can also reassure him that if he really wants to stop as badly as he says he does, he will probably succeed.

Telling him that he should have considered the consequences before he became addicted (B) serves no purpose other than making this person feel more miserable and depressed than he already is. Such a statement also tends to sever any lines of communication that may have been established and to prevent you from having a beneficial effect on the young man, no matter what further action is taken. You cannot alienate a patient and then expect to have a therapeutic effect on him. Similarly, reporting him to the police (E) will also eliminate you from a possibly beneficial role in his rehabilitation. Furthermore, it is likely that the police will not be particularly enthusiastic about your report. The police, for the most part, are not as concerned about the heroin addict as they are with his sources of supply. They would rather see an addict rehabilitated than jailed, and would probably refer this young man to some type of treatment center; you could do this yourself without involving the police.

Referring this man to a methadone maintenance program

(C) is a step in the right direction; however, a person who has been addicted for only six months should not be placed in a drug program that will continue his drug dependence for the rest of his life. Methadone maintenance should be considered for a person only if a program of withdrawal has been shown to lead repeatedly to relapse. One should initially attempt to refer him to a methadone withdrawal program (D). There is a possibility that such a young man would have good results in a properly designed methadone withdrawal program. To be effective, the program should include appropriate counseling and support. In such a program, this man's motivation and willingness to quit might be supported, and he might be counseled to change his circle of friends. Such a program would probably enable him to withdraw from heroin use and to remain unaddicted.

Referring this young man to a therapeutic community (F) may be an appropriate decision. As was mentioned earlier, this decision depends a great deal upon who is responsible for the therapeutic community, how the young man feels about it, and how you feel about it. But as with any referral, you should know the community very well before sending a person there for help.

Additional case histories and discussions of their solutions follow.

CASE 1-2

A thirty-six year-old woman is referred to you by the police because of her stated desire to "kick" the heroin habit. She is no stranger to the police, who report to you that she has been arrested numerous times on various charges, including prostitution and narcotics violations; has an eighteen-year history of heroin addiction; and has been to the federal treatment facility at Lexington, Kentucky, three times.

When she comes in, you see that she is an attractive and well-dressed woman who appears in no acute distress. When you ask her what brought her to see you, she replies that she is out on bail on a charge of prostitution, on the condition that she seek treatment for her addiction. During the course of the interview, she reveals that she had her last "fix" (injection of heroin) two hours ago and that she has been addicted to heroin since she was eighteen years old. Since that time, she has been "clean" four times. Three of these times were after going to Lexington. During these times she was once "clean" for four months, once for three months, and once for six weeks. The fourth time was for two-and-a-half years, while she was in jail. Each time, however, she started "shooting up" as soon as she returned to her old neighborhood and friends. She denies abuse of any other drugs, saying that she has always been able to raise the $50 to $100 a day to support her habit and that nothing else was ever as good as heroin. When you ask about alcohol, she says that she'd rather "be sick" (have withdrawal symptoms) than drink.

When you ask her why she wants to quit, she replies that she's tired of the whole thing. Her boyfriend of the past two years, also a heroin addict, died of an overdose four months ago, she reports. Since then, she says, she has become tired

THE NARCOTIC ANALGESICS

of hustling for her dope. She would like to relax and enjoy some of the good things in life, instead of winding up like her boyfriend. But she reports that she can't quit on her own. She has tried many times recently, but has only been able to go a few days until she starts shooting again. Then she begins crying and begs you to help her.

In this situation, what would you do?

(A) Refer this woman to a methadone withdrawal program.

(B) Refer this woman to a methadone maintenance program.

(C) Tell her that if she really wants to stop she doesn't need help from you, but can do it herself.

(D) Report to the police that nothing can be done for this woman and that she belongs in jail.

(E) Give her a talk about the evils and dangers of narcotic addiction.

(F) Suggest the following (write your own solution to the problem):

. . . .

. . . .

. . . .

. . . .

DISCUSSION

Giving this woman a talk about the evils and dangers of narcotic addiction (E) is certainly not necessary. Having been an addict for eighteen years, she probably knows more about the personal disadvantages of narcotic addiction than you do. Reporting to the police that nothing can be done for this person and that she belongs in jail (D) is not a judgment that you can or should make at this point. Even though this woman has in the past been either unable or unwilling to change, she deserves another chance. She has asked for your help and to report negatively to the police is no help at all. It is an abdication of professional responsibility. While (D) may be necessary, such a judgment can be made only after you have tried to help her in every way possible.

Telling her that if she really wants to stop she doesn't need you but could do it herself (C) is half right. In order to recover from an addiction, it is necessary to have a great deal of determination and motivation. But most of the time this alone is not enough. And at this point you can be of assistance. A methadone withdrawal program (A) is one form of assistance. The alleviation of physical discomfort of withdrawal by methadone, in conjunction with a program of counseling and support to help in overcoming estrangement from normal life, is often effective in withdrawing an addict from narcotics.

This woman's main problem, however, is not withdrawal. She has withdrawn completely four times, but each time has become addicted again. The problem is that narcotic addicts often have only other narcotic addicts as friends. And if and when a former addict returns to his friends and a drug environment it is very difficult for him to resist the peer pressure (and his own craving) toward addiction.

For these reasons, a methadone maintenance program (B) would seem most beneficial for this woman. It would remove her craving and enable her to better withstand the temptation to regress to addiction, for even if she did "shoot up" again, she would get no thrill from it. A methadone maintenance program would also remove the financial burden of supporting an addiction. This program, coupled with appropriate psychological support and counseling, might make it possible for her to find a more socially acceptable way of earning a living.

CASE 1-3

A sixteen year-old high school junior comes to see you because he knows your son. When asked what brings him to see you, he shows you several large, ulcerated, and infected lesions on his thighs. At first he denies any knowledge of the cause of these lesions, but after securing a promise from you that you won't tell his parents, he admits that he has been "popping" (injecting subcutaneously) heroin two or three times a week for several months. He came to see you, he says, because he is afraid of losing control and getting "strung-out" (addicted and in need of high doses), and also because the sores on his legs have frightened him. He feels that he wants to stop using heroin, but he is not sure that he can do so without help.

When asked how all this began, he replies that at first he just did it to see what would happen. He was at a party and most of the kids there were using heroin. He has a fear of needles and hypodermics in general, but he says that he found heroin was so "groovy" that he could overcome his fear of needles in order to use it.

He reports that heroin makes all of his problems go away for a while. When he takes the drug, he doesn't "hurt" any more. He spends all of his allowance on the drug, he says, and would probably spend more if he had it, but he doesn't want to steal or "break the law" to raise money.

When you ask him to tell you more about his problems, he replies that it's basically his parents. He says that his father and mother are always picking on him and are always critical of everything he does. His father is an engineer, and his mother is a housewife. He has two younger sisters, one is twelve and the other is ten years old. He says that his father is always giving him trouble about the length of his hair and the way he dresses and that his mother is always asking him why he can't be a nice boy and listen to his mother and father. His father is always ranting and raving about the "hippie punks" and "longhaired degenerates," he says, and all of this just "tears him up inside."

In addition to securing medical treatment for the sores on his leg, what would you do?

(A) Report him to the police as a narcotic addict.

(B) Tell him that if he doesn't stop you'll inform his parents.

(C) Suggest that if he had listened to his parents none of this would have happened and tell him that he should listen to them in the future.

(D) Ask him to try to avoid using the drug and to come back and talk to you again in a week, and tell him that you'll try to work this out with him.

(E) Suggest that this is a family problem and that if it would be all right with him, you would like to talk some more with him and also with his parents.

(F) Suggest the following (write your own solution):

. . . .

. . . .

. . . .

. . . .

DISCUSSION

Reporting him to the police as a narcotic addict (A) is totally inappropriate in this situation. Although some laws may have been broken, primary concern should be with this young man's welfare. It would be in his best interest to be treated as an ill person rather than as a criminal. While he may be psychologically dependent on heroin, it is questionable whether he is an addict as we have defined addiction. This point is especially important, as a diagnosis of addiction is, in our society, irreversible. It remains in the medical record and in the conscience of the patient as a permanent blemish. Finally, reporting him to the police is a betrayal of his trust in you.

Telling him that if he doesn't stop you'll inform his parents (B) is unwise. This is a threat that you will betray a trust given in confidence. It is similar to the tactics used by his parents, identifies you with them, and only aggravates the problem by increasing the pressures he feels. Furthermore, it eliminates you from any possible beneficial role.

Suggesting that none of this would have happened if he had listened to his parents and that he should listen to them in the future (C), although probably a true statement, completely ignores the reality of the situation. This adolescent is sensitive to the criticisms of his parents and is very unhappy that he doesn't please them; however, it is normal at this age to disagree with parents and to assert independence in style of dress and thought. Adolescence is characterized by rebellion and disagreement. Indeed, a passive, totally obedient and docile sixteen-year-old should be suspected of being emotionally ill. What is abnormal in this case is that the pressures have made him liable to inappropriate and dangerous behavior.

Asking him to try to avoid using the drug, and to come back and talk to you again in a week and telling him that you'll try to work it out with him (D) is definitely on the right track. There are some problems, however, in taking this course. Most states have laws prohibiting the treatment of minors without their parents' consent. This law often places you in a dilemma. Furthermore, although this is basically the young man's problem, a satisfactory resolution would be much more likely if you secure the cooperation and aid of the entire family.

Suggesting that this is a family problem and that if it would be all right with him, you would like to talk some more with him and also with his parents (E) seems to be the best alternative. This arranges for further interviews, and the suggestion also takes cognizance that this is a family problem. The main caution here is not to force the issue or to make further visits conditional upon either the cessation of drug use or the participation of his parents. He probably would like very much for his parents to be more understanding and in a better position to help him solve his problems.

The most important therapeutic tool here is a trusting relationship between you and this adolescent. Once this has been established, it may become easier to get the concerned parties together to resolve the problems and pressures of adolescent rebellion in a more appropriate and rational manner. In this case, however, the counselor must recognize that a favorable outcome is doubtful.

Even though physical dependence may not have occurred, the actuality of first-hand acquaintance with the effects of heroin will tend to undermine all efforts to counsel. Why has this adolescent come for help *at this particular time?* Very likely because he feels himself to be on the verge of a "mainlining" habit. If this is the case, the counselor is really being asked to step in and prevent this from happening. From a practical therapeutic standpoint this can seldom be attempted without resort to a residential treatment program, for only in such a program can there be physical control. In this type of case, counseling without such physical control will inevitably increase the adolescent's anxiety as the problems are brought to the fore. When this happens his first impulse may be to reach for the needle. Medical use of a safe, long-acting narcotic antagonist might be of help in this case, but unfortunately such a drug has not yet been developed.

As a final note of pessimistic realism, we must consider the possibility that this adolescent has already been "mainlining," but is trying to cover this up as a kind of psychological denial of his imminent addiction. Although this would be important to discern, the counseling problem would be approached in a manner similar to that described above.

CASE 1-4

A twenty-three year-old man comes to see you about withdrawing from heroin. He says he has been "shooting" for a year and a half, but he is afraid of losing control and getting really "strung out." He seems calm. You ask him when he had his last dose, and he replies that two hours ago he shot "two dimes and a quarter," or two injections of $10 and one of $25 worth of heroin. He reports that he has "kicked" twice before, once when he was "clean" for about six weeks with the help of some tranquilizers a doctor gave him, and once when he had hepatitis and was in the hospital for a month. He reports that during these times his craving for heroin itself was not as bad as his craving for the "spike" (needle). He would have dreams at night about syringes and needles, and sometimes he would inject himself with water or even just his own blood, just to feel the needle in his arm. He becomes quite animated as he describes the feeling of putting the needle in, seeing blood in the syringe,[10] and pushing the plunger down. He says that after a while he just couldn't take it anymore and started shooting heroin again.

He also says that he heard methadone stops the craving for heroin, and he asks if you could give him some methadone to help him "kick" his heroin habit.

In this situation what would you do?

(A) Refer him to a methadone withdrawal program.
(B) Refer him to a methadone maintenance program.
(C) Suggest the following (write your own solution):

. . . .

. . . .

. . . .

. . . .

. . . .

DISCUSSION

Involving this man in a methadone withdrawal program (A) is not enough. He has been withdrawn before and has relapsed. Similarly, a methadone maintenance program (B) will probably not solve his problems, because much more is involved here than simply a narcotic addiction. Although a withdrawal program will withdraw this man and a maintenance program will block his craving for narcotics, neither will affect his "needle habit," his pathological fixation with the act of injecting himself. This is a manifestation of a very serious personality disturbance that is beyond the scope of the counseling and support measures associated with methadone programs. Intensive psychotherapy is indicated in this case, perhaps on an in-patient basis. But even then, the prospects of rehabilitation may be slim.

Some authorities consider needle fixation to be a form of sexual perversion that is almost unrelated to the drug addiction itself. So even though a maintenance program can block both the craving for narcotics and the effects of an injection of heroin, such a person would probably soon turn to intravenously injecting some other drug, such as amphetamines or cocaine.

Such cases are not common, and there is no easy or pat solution to this problem. Even intensive psychotherapy during confinement in an institution may not be enough in this case. But it is important for an advisor or physician to try to help everyone and to suggest the help which is most likely to achieve rehabilitation.

NOTES

1. J. H. Jaffe, "Drug Addiction and Drug Abuse," in *The Pharmacological Basis of Therapeutics,* 4th edition, ed. L. S. Goodman and A. Gilman (New York: Macmillan Company, 1970), p. 277.

2. *New York Times,* 23 September 1969, p. 34.

3. V. P. Dole, M. E. Nyswander, and A. Warner, "Successful Treatment of 750 Criminal Addicts," *Journal of the American Medical Association* 206, no. 12 (16 December 1968): 2708.

4. *The Drug Takers,* Time-Life Special Report, ed. N. P. Ross (1965), p. 13.

5. A. Wikler *et al.,* "Effects of Frontal Lobotomy on the Morphine Abstinence Syndrome in Man: An Experimental Study," *AMA Archives of Neurology and Psychiatry* 67, no. 4 (April 1952): 520–21.

6. D. B. Louria, T. Hensle, and J. Rose, "The Major Medical Complications of Heroin Addiction," *Annals of Internal Medicine* 67, no. 1 (July 1967): 18.

7. E. Freese, "Structure-Activity Considerations in Potential Mutagenicity," in *Drugs of Abuse: Their Genetic and Other Chronic Non-Psychiatric Hazards,* ed. S. S. Epstein (Cambridge, Mass.: M.I.T. Press, 1971), p. 123.

8. J. H. Jaffe, "Narcotic Analgesics," in *The Pharmacological Basis of Therapeutics,* 4th edition, p. 243.

9. C. E. Cherubin, "The Medical Sequelae of Narcotic Addiction," *Annals of Internal Medicine* 67, no. 1 (July 1967): 25.

10. Prior to injection of a drug, an addict usually pulls back on the plunger of the syringe to see if the needle is in the vein. If it is, blood will appear in the syringe.

Chapter 2
ALCOHOL

Alcohol has been used as an intoxicant since prehistoric times and still retains a similar place in contemporary civilization. There are an estimated seventy to seventy-five million consumers of alcohol in this country, and every year over ten billion dollars is spent on alcoholic beverages.[1] Although moderate use of alcohol is widely accepted in our society, the effects of both acute and chronic alcohol intoxication can be tragic. Alcohol is acknowledged to be a causal factor in one-half of all automobile accidents fatal to drivers;[2] and in a study of 2,500 pedestrians killed in highway accidents, 31 percent were found to be under the influence of alcohol.[3] According to other studies, alcohol is involved in 27 to 30 percent of all violent deaths.[4] But this is only part of the price our society pays for the abuse of alcohol. The loss in potential wages, and the costs in medical and custodial care, crimes and accidents, and just plain human misery are too great to estimate. And estimates are that from four to six million individuals in this country are alcoholics.[5]

The term "alcoholism" is used to indicate the condition of addiction to alcohol. The AMA Committee on Alcoholism defines the condition as a "highly complex illness characterized by preoccupation with alcohol and loss of control over its consumption such as to lead usually to intoxication if drinking is begun; by chronicity; by progression; and by a tendency toward relapse. It is typically associated with physical disability and impaired emotional, occupational, and/or social adjustments as a direct consequence of persistent and excessive use of alcohol."[6]

Alcohol is a central nervous system (CNS) depressant. Although the effects of low doses may seem to be stimulating, this is because inhibitory centers in the CNS are depressed first. A shy person, for example, may become very talkative after a few drinks. This depression of inhibitions may be interpreted as stimulation. However, low doses of alcohol increase neither mental nor physical abilities, except where inhibitions prevent optimum performance.

Alcohol is absorbed from the stomach, to some extent, and completely and rapidly from the proximal small intestine. The alcohol is fairly uniformly distributed throughout the body. The effects of acohol on the mind and body are roughly proportional to the blood concentration, i.e., the amount of alcohol present in the blood. However, the effects are more marked at a given blood concentration, when the amount of alcohol in the blood is rising, than at the *same* concentration, when the amount in the blood is falling. Furthermore, straight whiskey on an empty stomach will be absorbed faster and will give a higher peak blood concentration than the same amount of whiskey taken with food or an equivalent amount of alcohol consumed as beer.

Alcohol in the blood stream causes many disturbances of nervous function. These include increased production of urine that is mediated by the pituitary gland, flushing, a feeling of warmth due to inhibition of nervous control of small blood vessels, and lowered body temperature due to an effect on the temperature regulator in the brain. Alcohol also stimulates the secretion of stomach acid.

Of the alcohol in the blood, 90 to 98 percent is oxidized in the liver. The average rate of oxidation in a non-tolerant individual is low, approximately 10 ml/hour. In an individual who has developed a tolerance to alcohol, the *maximum* rate of oxidation does not exceed 400 to 500 ml/day, or only approximately twice the average rate in the nontolerant individual. This is related to the tolerant individual's ability to consume greater amounts of alcohol than the nontolerant individual.

Although small amounts of alcohol consumed intermittently have not been shown to produce deleterious physical consequences, alcoholics are susceptible to many illnesses. Some of the physical effects related to chronic consumption of large amounts of alcohol are numbness and sometimes paralysis of the limbs (peripheral neuropathies); pellagra (a B-vitamin deficiency disease); a type of blindness (nutritional amblyopia); confusion, stupor, and double vision (Wernicke's encephalopathy); chronic memory loss (Korsakoff's psychosis); and fatty degeneration and cirrhosis of the liver. Such illnesses appear to be due to a combination of nutritional deficiencies and the direct effect of alcohol on the body. Furthermore, one-third of all heavy drinkers have chronic gastritis. Pancreatitis; gastro-intestinal hemorrhage, due to perforated ulcers; pneumonia; and head injuries due to falls are frequent medical complications of heavy drinking and acute intoxication.

Another effect of chronic alcohol consumption is the development of physical dependence and consequently, upon cessation of consumption, a withdrawal syndrome. Actually, with alcohol there is a spectrum of withdrawal syndromes, depending upon the degree of physical dependence that has developed. The first signs of withdrawal consist mostly of acute tremulousness and anxiety ("shakes" and "jitters"). The mildest syndrome stops there. However, some withdrawals include transient visual and auditory hallucinations or even acute alcoholic hallucinosis. Also, grand mal convulsive seizures ("rum fits") and delirium tremens ("the DT's") may occur.

Delirium tremens is a very serious medical complication that goes beyond the more common tremulousness and anxiety, and has a grave prognosis (death in 10 to 20 percent of the cases). It is characterized by excessive motor and speech activity, autonomic overactivity (sweating, rapid heart rate, fever, dilated pupils), disorientation and confusion, and disordered sensory perception. The cause of death in delirium tremens is usually loss of blood pressure (vascular collapse), high fever (hyperthermia), or associated injury or infection. The treatment of delirium tremens is non-specific and supportive in nature. Treatment should always be carried out in a hospital. But to date, it has been very difficult, if not impossible, to reduce significantly the occurrence or severity of DT's by the use of any drugs during the withdrawal period.

Although many have tried, no one has been able to define the "alcoholic personality." Indeed, most authorities deny its existence. Psychological factors are of the utmost importance in understanding alcoholism, but they fail to answer all the questions raised about its etiology and progression. However, a history of early emotional deprivation, contributing to immature ways of dealing with feelings of anxiety, hostility, inferiority, and depression, seem common among alcoholics. Parental relationships also seem significant. Often there is the development in childhood of a passive, dependent type of character. It is not known why some people cope with their feelings and pressures by abusing alcohol. However, alcoholism may be thought of as a learned pattern of coping with feelings and social pressures by self-intoxication with alcohol.

Several specific alcoholism treatment programs have been developed. Many of these include either individual or group psychotherapy. Alcoholics Anonymous, the most widely known program, requires an individual to acknowledge he is an alcoholic, to agree he needs help, and to say he wants to recover. Once the alcoholic has taken these steps, he can join what is actually a cooperative effort of all the members of the program to help each other achieve and maintain sobriety. The goal of AA is complete abstinence from alcohol, and many of its members display an almost evangelical fervor concerning their organization. Another program is that of the Salvation Army. Both the Salvation Army and Alcoholics Anonymous advocate adherence to a religious belief as an important additional means of control over alcoholism. Each program has demonstrated its own value and success, but no single program exists that is best for every alcoholic. With a problem as complex as alcoholism, many different strategies are necessary.

An adjunct to the treatment of alcoholism is the drug disulfiram (Antabuse). Disulfiram interferes with one step in the oxidation of alcohol. When an individual has been taking disulfiram, ingestion of alcohol in any form will make him violently ill. He will have flushing, nausea, vomiting, and often fainting. This effect will persist from six to fourteen days after the last dose of disulfiram. The advantages of this drug are that a decision to resist temptation and remain abstinent must be made only once a day, rather than several times a day, and that a decision to resume drinking must be made one or two weeks in advance. However, disulfiram is an aid to will-power, not a substitute for it.

Anyone who attempts to treat alcoholism encounters many problems. The time to treat alcoholism is not when medical problems, such as cirrhosis of the liver, have developed, nor after the behavior pattern has persisted for a prolonged period; rather, treatment should be undertaken as soon as a drinking problem begins to manifest itself. However, the chief defense mechanisms used by alcoholics, denial (acting as if there is no problem) and rationalization (making excuses), interfere with therapy. A therapist usually encounters severe resistance from the alcoholic, and often becomes angry and frustrated because of his seeming inability to have a therapeutic effect on his patient. Low-pressure tactics must be used. Because there is no single cause of alcoholism, any treatment program that deals with only one aspect of causation is inevitably doomed to failure. But alcoholism *is* treatable. The aim of treatment should be to control the problem. The alcoholic must learn to deal effectively with his environment and his problems without alcohol. In fact, he must learn a new style of living.

QUESTIONS

1. Delirium tremens is a condition representing acute alcoholic intoxication.

    True or false? . . . . . .

2. To reach a given level of anesthesia, an alcoholic patient will require higher doses of general anesthetics than will a non-alcoholic patient.

    True or false? . . . . . .

3. An alcoholic always drinks more than a social drinker.

    True or false? . . . . . .

4. Alcoholics have the same life expectancy as non-alcoholics.

    True or false? . . . . . .

5. The behavior pattern of alcoholism is untreatable.

    True or false? . . . . . .

6. Alcohol and "sleeping pills" have cumulative effects.

    True or false? . . . . . .

7. Alcohol has almost no caloric value whatsoever.

    True or false? . . . . . .

8. Alcoholism is an inherited disease.

    True or false? . . . . . .

9. There is no relation between the amount of alcohol in-

gested and the level of alcohol in the blood.

True or false? . . . . . .

10. It is possible to "drink all night" and not become intoxicated.

True or false? . . . . . .

11. Alcohol makes you feel warm by raising your body temperature.

True or false? . . . . . .

12. It is possible to delineate the "alcoholic personality."

True or false? . . . . . .

13. Alcohol improves sexual function.

True or false? . . . . . .

ANSWERS

1. Delirium tremens is a situation representing acute alcoholic intoxication.

Answer: *False.* Delirium tremens is an alcoholic withdrawal syndrome. It is not an intoxication, nor is it caused by any vitamin or nutritional deficiency. It is usually preceded by an abrupt cessation of alcohol intake after a period of six to seven weeks of heavy drinking. Withdrawal syndromes in general, and delirium tremens in particular, are often seen among alcoholic patients whose alcoholism is unknown to the attending physician and who are admitted to the hospital for such medical conditions as pneumonia or accidental trauma arising during a period of acute intoxication. These patients typically experience withdrawal syndromes within two to three days after hospital admission (and their last drink), thus seriously complicating their medical treatment.

2. To reach a given level of anesthesia, an alcoholic patient will require higher doses of general anesthetics than will a non-alcoholic patient.

Answer: *True.* This phenomenon is called cross-tolerance. Alcohol demonstrates cross-tolerance to general anesthetics and other general depressants, such as barbiturates. However, it must be kept in mind that with all of these agents, even though a larger amount of drug is required to reach a given level of depression, there is no marked elevation of the lethal dose. This is often a factor in accidental deaths from an inadvertent overdose of general depressants.

43

3. An alcoholic always drinks more than a social drinker.

Answer: *False*. Most alcoholics consume more alcohol than most social drinkers, but this is not the key factor in alcoholism. The behavior pattern of the individual is more important than the amount of alcohol consumed. The alcoholic drinks for the sole purpose of intoxication. He organizes his life around drinking and copes with his problems of personal adjustment by becoming intoxicated. Some social drinkers consume large amounts of alcohol, but their behavior patterns do not classify them as alcoholics. However, many alcoholics rationalize their behavior as social drinking, even when this is no longer the case. Sometimes it becomes very difficult to determine where social drinking ends and alcoholism begins.

4. Alcoholics have the same life expectancy as non-alcoholics.

Answer: *False*. Alcoholics are particularly susceptible to pneumonia, tuberculosis, head injuries from falls, gastrointestinal problems, and neurological problems, as a result of both acute intoxication with and chronic ingestion of alcohol. The life expectancy of an alcoholic is approximately twelve years less than that of a non-alcoholic.

5. The behavior pattern of alcoholism is untreatable.

Answer: *False*. Although the treatment of the alcoholic presents many problems, both for the patient and the counselor, the behavior patterns involved can be changed. However, the therapeutic aim should be the control of behavior, rather than an often unobtainable cure. The patient must learn to deal effectively with his environment and his problems without alcohol. This involves acquiring a new life style, which is difficult for any person.

6. Alcohol and "sleeping pills" have cumulative effects.

Answer: *True*. An all too common cause of accidental death is respiratory depression due to an inadvertent overdose of general depressants. The respiration of a person intoxicated with alcohol is already depressed. When such a person then takes a sleeping agent, such as a barbiturate, he may further depress his respiration to the lethal point.

7. Alcohol has almost no caloric value whatsoever.

Answer: *False*. The oxidation of alcohol provides seven kilocalories per gram, but no protein or vitamins. Alcohol provides the total caloric intake for some alcoholics, a situation that leads to the nutritional deficiencies commonly seen in alcoholic patients.

8. Alcoholism is an inherited disease.

Answer: *False*. There is no evidence that supports this assertion.

9. There is no relation between the amount of alcohol ingested and the level of alcohol in the blood.

Answer: *False*. There is a direct relationship between the blood level of alcohol and the amount ingested. However, the alcohol concentration in the blood is influenced by many factors. For example, four ounces of whiskey ingested on an empty stomach will lead to a blood concentration (level) of from 67 to 92 mg percent (milligrams per 100 cubic centimeters). When the same amount of alcohol is taken with a mixed meal, the resultant blood level will be from 30 to 53 mg percent. A person whose blood level of alcohol is over 150 mg percent (100 mg percent in some cases) is legally considered under the influence of alcohol. A person whose blood level of alcohol is under 50 mg percent is legally considered not under the influence of alcohol. The determination of intoxication of a person whose blood level is between 50 and 150 mg percent is based on other factors. However, according to one study, automobile drivers with a blood level of 150 mg percent were found to be thirty-three times more likely to have an accident than were people with no alcohol in their bloodstreams.[7] Furthermore, a blood alcohol level of 150 mg percent has a greater effect when the blood level is rising than when the blood level is falling.

10. It is possible to "drink all night" and not become intoxicated.

Answer: *True*. The average person is able to metabolize approximately one ounce of whiskey per hour. Therefore, if one consumes no more than this amount, one can literally drink all night without becoming intoxicated. For example, let us take the hypothetical situation of an intoxicated man with a blood level of alcohol of 150 mg percent and a maximum metabolic oxidation rate of one ounce of whiskey per hour. If this intoxicated person continues drinking whiskey at a rate of 0.9 ounces per hour, his blood level of alcohol will fall, and he will gradually become more and more sober. However, if he consumes whiskey at a rate of 1.1 ounces per hour, his blood level will rise, and he will gradually become more and more intoxicated.

11. Alcohol makes you feel warm by raising your body temperature.

Answer: *False*. Alcohol causes a feeling of warmth by dilating the blood vessels in the skin. This, however, leads to an increased loss of heat from the body; in certain situations, this can be dangerous.

12. It is possible to delineate the "alcoholic personality."

Answer: *False*. Although alcoholics often have many characteristics in common, the underlying personalities and motives for alcoholism are as numerous as the number of alcoholics. Trying to delineate the "alcoholic personality" is as fruitless a task as trying to delineate the non-alcoholic personality. All of our insights into why any person becomes an alcoholic are retrospective ones; and unfortunately, such insights have little or no predictive value.

13. Alcohol improves sexual function.

Answer: *False*. Shakespeare, in Macbeth (Act 2, Scene 3), accurately enumerates the effects of alcohol:

Macduff: What three things does drink especially provoke?

Porter: Marry, sir, nose-painting, sleep, and urine. Lechery, sir, it provokes and unprovokes; it provokes the desire, but it takes away the performance. . . .

CASE 2-1

A thirty-one year-old woman who comes to see you reports that her husband drinks too much and asks that you talk to him and "help him overcome his problems." Upon further questioning, she tells you he is a thirty-seven year-old junior executive who works for an advertising firm. They have two children and have been married for ten years. She says he often comes home from work in a nasty mood, makes snide remarks to her, and sometimes shouts at or slaps the children. He has usually had several drinks before he gets home; and as soon as he comes in the door, he pours himself another drink. Sometimes he will not even eat dinner but will sit in front of the television and drink until he passes out. She also reports that they are not being invited to parties any more because he always gets drunk and makes a scene. When you ask how long things have been going this way, she says her husband has always been a heavy drinker but that two years ago he was passed up for a promotion in his firm and that a younger man was chosen instead, and that things really started to deteriorate after that. You agree to talk to the husband, and he reluctantly comes to your office. He denies that there is any problem but says it's just that his wife thinks he drinks too much. He says he has always been able to hold his liquor well. He complains that his wife is always nagging him to make more money, constantly comparing him with her friends' husbands, and always wanting more and more things. It is very difficult for them to make ends meet. Further questioning reveals that he feels his wife ignores him and is always doing things for the children and has no time for him. He refuses to go into detail about his drinking habits, and says that he just likes to drink but could stop whenever he wanted to.

In this situation, what would you do?

(A) Tell him that he is an alcoholic and refer him to Alcoholics Anonymous.
(B) Suggest that he stop drinking for health reasons.
(C) Tell him that he's ruining his life and making his wife and children miserable.
(D) Suggest that both he and his wife seek family counseling.
(E) Suggest that he and his wife get a divorce.
(F) Suggest the following (write your own solution):

. . . .

. . . .

. . . .

. . . .

. . . .

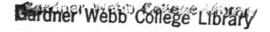

DISCUSSION

Telling him that he is an alcoholic and referring him to Alcoholics Anonymous (A) will probably not help in this case. This man denies that he has a drinking problem and will not believe you if you tell him he is an alcoholic (although he may be). Furthermore, Alcoholics Anonymous accepts only those who admit that they are alcoholics and who want to do something about it. This man will do neither. And advising him to stop drinking for health reasons (B) is skirting the main issue. This man has severe emotional problems and is very unlikely to respond to such patronizing advice.

Telling him that he is ruining his life and making his wife and children miserable (C) may make you feel better, but it won't help him. He probably already knows this and feels guilty about it. You will succeed only in making him feel more guilty and may even aggravate his drinking problem. Suggesting that he and his wife get a divorce (E) is precipitous advice at this point. Although it may be that a divorce is the best solution to this family's problem, such a decision should be made only after thoughtful consideration of all other possible alternatives.

Suggesting that he and his wife seek family counseling (D) is the best choice here. Although it may seem like "passing the buck," unless you are willing and able to spend many hours with this couple and endure much frustration and disappointment in the process, you had better refer them to someone who is able to commit himself to such counseling.

Furthermore, the referral itself may be a long and arduous procedure. There is no way to force this couple to seek help. A therapeutic program of family counseling would have to involve both the husband and wife and would concern itself primarily with resolving the marital difficulties.

The term "family counseling" is used to emphasize that it is not necessarily an academic degree that determines the competence of the counselor. A psychiatrist, psychologist, social worker, clergyman, or marriage counselor may be able to provide the therapy the family needs. What is important is that the counselor have both the temperament for and experience in handling such problems.

In this case the history of the marital relationship and its current status will have to be understood. The wife's attitude will be of critical importance. The wife whose loyalty is unflagging, "no matter what happens," may be unconsciously protecting the husband's denial. However, a therapist cannot attack such a behavior pattern head-on. Furthermore, such a couple may fail to get help even from the most skilled therapist. On the other hand, if it turns out that the wife has been seriously considering divorce, there is a chance that the husband may overcome his denial enough to get started in a rehabilitation program. The threat of divorce can sometimes be effective, but only if the spouse has actually been fulfilling some of the alcoholic's dependency needs *and* only when the spouse is serious and not simply wielding an empty threat.

CASE 2-2

A physician asks you to see a forty-six year-old man who has been hospitalized. The patient stated that he was well until he noticed that his skin and the whites of his eyes were turning yellow and that his ankles, legs, and abdomen were becoming swollen. He went to his physician, who told him he had cirrhosis of the liver and arranged for his admission to the hospital. His hospital course has been unremarkable, and his jaundice (yellow skin), edema (fluid in the tissues), and ascites (fluid in the abdomen) are slowly resolving. His physician has told him that he will survive the cirrhosis and can go home in two weeks, but that if he doesn't stop drinking he will die within a few years.

When you go to see him, you find a man who looks malnourished. He has thin arms and a swollen abdomen. He is in a private room. He says that he feels all right now and never did feel very bad, and that he's looking forward to going home. He is a vice-president of a large company and lives in one of the more expensive and exclusive suburbs in the area. When you ask him what he thinks the cirrhosis is due to, he replies that his doctor said it was because he drinks too much, but that he really doesn't think that is the whole story. When you ask him to elaborate, he goes on to say he really doesn't drink very much. He'll have a few drinks with lunch, then a few before dinner, and a few more in the evening. He says he has never had much of an appetite and has always been thin, but has always eaten well. He says he began drinking at eighteen and drank more when he was young than he does now.

When you ask him what he is going to do after he is dis-

charged from the hospital, he replies, "Oh, I guess I'll have to cut down on my drinking. Doctor's orders, you know."
In this situation what would you do?

(A) Tell him that he is an alcoholic and refer him to Alcoholics Anonymous.
(B) Tell him that if he doesn't stop drinking he'll die within a few years.
(C) Tell him and his physician that he's a hopeless case.
(D) Tell him that if he has any problems stopping drinking, he can always come to you for help.
(E) Tell him that he belongs in a special hospital until he can stop drinking.
(F) Suggest the following (write your own solution):

. . . .

. . . .

. . . .

. . . .

. . . .

DISCUSSION

Telling him that he is an alcoholic and referring him to Alcoholics Anonymous (A) would probably not help in this case. This man, like the man in the previous case, denies that he has a drinking problem and will not believe you if you tell him that he is an alcoholic. Alcoholics Anonymous accepts only those who admit they have a problem with drinking and who are motivated to do something about it.

Telling him that if he doesn't stop drinking he'll die within a few years (B) is not likely to do much good in this case. If you made this choice, you are underestimating the alcoholic's power of denial. The very deterioration of his physical condition escaped his notice until he reached this extreme state. This man's physician has already confronted him to no avail. If you merely repeat the warning, this man will just act as if you are talking about somebody else and not about him. Scare tactics usually are not a good tool in the treatment of alcoholics.

Telling him that he belongs in a special hospital until he can stop drinking (E) is not a practical choice. This man denies that he has a drinking problem and will not voluntarily commit himself to further hospitalization. Having him committed against his will may not be legally possible; but, even if it were possible, such action could arouse great hostility in this man. Such hostility could easily subvert any proposed treatment program.

Telling him and his physician that he is a hopeless case (C) may not be far from the truth, but such a remark seldom helps a patient. In fact there always is hope. Occasionally the "hopeless" alcoholic cures or controls his addiction when

54

grave illness is imminent. But in this case, all you can do is offer your services in the future.

Telling him that if he has any problem stopping drinking he can always come to you for help (D) may not seem much of a choice. But it is the only one that you have in this situation. It is a sad fact that you can't force yourself on those who do not want your help. Unfortunately, those who need help the most are often those who resist it most vigorously.

Another approach to helping this person would involve working with his family. A skillful medical social worker could establish contacts with the spouse or other important family members or friends. The best time to do this is immediately after admission to the hospital. In this particular case it would not be surprising to find that one or more people are fully aware of his alcoholism yet shelter and maintain him in his "executive" position. Study of this patient's history could determine whether such a behavior pattern has been life-long (since age 18). Advice-giving in such a case is no simple matter. It would be appropriate for this patient's supporters to seek advice from an experienced professional whether or not the patient does so himself. They would then be in a better position to weigh the pros and cons of either maintaining the *status quo* or making a change in their relationships with this afflicted person.

CASE 2-3

A thirty-three year-old man comes to see you. He says he wants some information about drinking. When you ask him to tell you about what's bothering him, he reports that he started drinking when he was in the army. He enlisted at age eighteen and remained in the service for six years. He says that about all he did during this time was get married, drink, and get divorced. He has no children and has not remarried. He is now working regularly as a machinist. After work, he usually stops at a bar with the guys, and they'll have a few. He often stays longer at the bar than the others. When he gets home, he'll usually drink a six-pack or two of beer while watching television.

The incident that has brought him to see you occurred several weeks ago. An old army buddy came to town on a Friday, and he had just been paid. They went to a bar together and started drinking and talking about old times. He says that the next thing he remembers is waking up in a cheap hotel in a city a hundred miles away. He was broke, hung over, and dirty. It was Monday morning, his buddy was gone, and he had absolutely no memory of what had happened to him over the weekend. When he got back home, some of his friends kidded him about the bender he had thrown. He says that this was the first time anything like this ever happened to him and that it really has him worried.

In this situation what would you do?

(A) Have him hospitalized and treated for alcoholism.

(B) Reassure him that he's got nothing to worry about, that it was just a wild spree that can happen to anyone.

56

(C) Tell him that if he doesn't stop drinking, he'll die.
(D) Ask him what he thinks about his drinking habits.
(E) Suggest that he get married and settle down.
(F) Suggest the following (write your own solution):

. . . .

. . . .

. . . .

. . . .

. . . .

DISCUSSION

Telling him that if he doesn't stop drinking he'll die (C) is true after a fashion, as everyone will die sooner or later and those who drink will probably die sooner. However, scare tactics are out of place here. This man is already frightened. Rather than frightening him even more, you should use this fear and concern for his own welfare as a channel through which you can develop a close, trusting, therapeutic relationship.

Reassuring him that he will probably be all right is a proper way to allay some of his fears and to begin developing a relationship. However, reassuring him to the point of telling him he has nothing to worry about and saying his episode was a wild spree that could happen to anyone (B) is going too far. He *does* have something to worry about, and he senses it. If you deny that he has a problem when he thinks he does, he will lose confidence in your ability to help him. This man experienced what is called a "blackout," a wild drinking spree associated with a total lack of recall about what occurred during the spree. It was literally a "lost weekend." Blackouts are a danger sign of impending alcoholism and should properly be considered a cause for alarm.

Getting married and settling down (E) may be just what this man needs. However, at this point you don't have enough information to make this judgment. Although marriage is a stabilizing influence for some men, keep in mind that bachelors have no monopoly on drinking problems.

Having him hospitalized and treated for alcoholism (A) may be just the thing this man needs at this point. Again, however, you do not have enough information at this time to make such a judgment. Therefore, asking him what he thinks about his drinking habits (D) is the proper choice. If this man says he is worried that he drinks too much, would like to stop but doesn't know if he can, and wants you to help him, then perhaps having him hospitalized (A) would be indicated. However, if he doesn't relate the blackout episode to a drinking problem, you will not be able to have him agree to hospitalization and must instead try to convince him of the relationship between his drinking habits and the blackout episode. You should also offer your help for the future.

There is no one way to deal with alcoholics or potential alcoholics. You must tailor your advice and your therapy to each individual and his case. In the best of situations there may be very little you can do; but to have any beneficial effect at all, your intervention must be appropriate to the situation. Any advice you give this man must be based upon a realistic appraisal of what responses you can expect from him. Such realism comes only with the development of a trusting relationship between you and the patient and with experience in working with alcoholics.

NOTES

1. J. H. Jaffe, "Drug Addiction and Drug Abuse," in *The Pharmacological Basis of Therapeutics,* 4th edition, ed. L. S. Goodman and A. Gilman (New York: Macmillan Company, 1970), p. 291.

2. *Manual of Alcoholism of the American Medical Association,* ed. Robert J. Shearer (n.p.: American Medical Association, 1968), p. 8.

3. T. A. Gonzales and A. Gettler, "Alcohol and the Pedestrian in Traffic Accidents," *Journal of the American Medical Association* 117, no. 18 (1 November 1941): 1525.

4. D. M. Spain, V. A. Bradess, and A. A. Eggston, "Alcohol and Violent Death: A One Year Study of Consecutive Cases in a Representative Community," *Journal of the American Medical Association* 146, no. 4 (26 May 1951): 335.

5. *Manual on Alcoholism,* p. 7.

6. *Ibid.,* p. 6.

7. R. C. Holcomb, "Alcohol in Relation to Traffic Accidents," *Journal of the American Medical Association* 111, no. 12 (17 September 1938): 1082.

Chapter 3

HYPNOTICS AND TRANQUILIZERS

Hypnotics, also known as soporifics and sedatives, are in a class of drugs called general depressants. They depress a wide range of biological functions in many organs. They are unspecific in their effect; but the central nervous system (CNS) is far more sensitive to these agents, in the doses normally used, than are other organs. Tranquilizers are of two classes: minor tranquilizers and major tranquilizers, or the intermediate and the special depressants.

The most common hypnotics are the barbiturates. Others include the bromide salts, chloral hydrate, paraldehyde, glutethimide (Doriden), and methyprylon (Noludar). There are many different barbiturates and literally scores of other hypnotic drugs available today. They may differ slightly in duration of action or particular side effects, but they all tend to resemble each other, and all share most of the disadvantages of barbiturates. Less is known about these agents, however, than is known about barbiturates, which are still the most useful and versatile of the hypnotic drugs.

Over eight hundred thousand pounds of barbiturates are produced every year in the United States; enough to fill over six billion 60 mg capsules.[1] The chief use of barbiturates is to produce sleep. They are thought to cause sleep by their depressant effect on the reticular activating system in the brain, which may be thought of as the brain's wakefulness center. However, the sleep induced by barbiturates is not identical to natural sleep. Natural sleep consists of alternating periods of deep sleep and paradoxical sleep (also known as REM or rapid eye movement sleep). As a succession of visual images, dreaming occurs during paradoxical sleep. Barbiturates reduce the amount and the proportion of time spent in paradoxical sleep. Some researchers feel that this may represent a deleterious side effect of these drugs. Another effect of barbiturates is what is called "drug hangover." This may be due to unmetabolized drug still circulating in the body, residual aftereffects of the drug on the brain, the deprivation of paradoxical sleep, or perhaps to some combination of these.

Barbiturates are not analgesics. They lack the ability to reduce pain without impairment of consciousness. Barbiturates also depress the respiratory control center of the brain. This causes the concentration of CO_2 in the blood to rise and the concentration of oxygen to fall. This effect is intensified by the concurrent use of barbiturates with alcohol, other general depressant drugs, or the narcotic analgesics. The depression of respiration is the chief cause of death in barbiturate poisoning.

In high doses, all of the hypnotics have an anticonvulsant effect. In addition, phenobarbital, in low doses, has an anticonvulsant effect unrelated to its sedative effect. This makes it a very useful drug in the treatment of such convulsive disorders as epilepsy. The barbiturates are also administered, in one-fourth to one-third the hypnotic dose, for sedation and relief of anxiety. However, this use has decreased since the introduction of the minor tranquilizers.

Although tolerance to barbiturates occurs, there is little concurrent elevation of the lethal dose. This is very important because the lethal dose of barbiturates is only about ten to fifteen times the hypnotic dose. A habitual user may become tolerant to the point of taking five to ten times the hypnotic dose, thereby tremendously increasing the chances of an accidental overdose.

All of the hypnotics can and have been abused. By far their most common route of administration is oral ingestion. Only rarely are they injected intravenously, probably because intravenous injection of these agents would in most cases produce unconsciousness rather than a "high." Furthermore, barbiturates are tissue irritants, which tend to produce abscesses at injection sites. Hypnotics produce an intoxication which is subjectively similar to that produced by alcohol. In fact, many alcoholics abuse these agents because they enable them to be "drunk" without the smell of alcohol on their breath.

Physical dependence, as well as psychological dependence and addiction, can develop with the use of the barbiturates. Physical dependence is closely related to the dose, the frequency, and the duration of use. It has been found that 200 mg of pentobarbital (Nembutal) can be taken every day for three months without the development of physical dependence.[2] The severity of the withdrawal syndrome is also related to the dose used. Abrupt withdrawal from high doses is characterized by tremulousness, anxiety, weakness, and insomnia. This can proceed into grand mal convulsive seizures and delirium, and may even be life-threatening. Furthermore, the convulsions associated with the barbiturate withdrawal syndrome are not prevented or alleviated by other antiepileptic drugs, such as diphenylhydantoin (Dilantin). The withdrawal of a patient from high doses of barbiturates is a serious problem in medical management. It should not be undertaken outside of a hospital, and it is best accomplished in a psychiatric hospital. The treatment consists of very gradual withdrawal, accompanied by appropriate medical and psychiatric supportive measures.

The minor tranquilizers are very similar to the hypnotic drugs. They include some of the drugs most frequently prescribed by doctors: chlordiazepoxide (Librium), diazepam (Valium), and meprobamate (Miltown, Equanil). They are used mainly for daytime sedation in patients who suffer from worry and tension. In these people they induce a degree of drowsiness and relief of anxiety similar to that produced by low doses of alcohol or barbiturates. Unlike the major tranquilizers, they have no special anti-psychotic effect. The main difference between the hypnotics and the minor tranquilizers, and the reason they are called intermediate depressants, is the ratio of the lethal dose to the minimal therapeutic dose. This is called the therapeutic ratio. For the hypnotics, this ratio ranges between twenty-five and forty to one; that is, the lethal dose may be twenty-five to forty times the amount of the minimal therapeutic dose. For meprobamate, the ratio is between sixty and a hundred to one; and the ratio may be even higher for chlordiazepoxide.

In the first six years of its use, only eight suicidal deaths due to meprobamate overdose were reported, although many more were attempted. This increased therapeutic ratio is the main reason the intermediate depressants are better suited as "tranquilizers" than are the hypnotics. But experimental evidence for the relative efficacy of these two classes of drugs in relieving anxiety in humans is, at the present time, ambiguous and contradictory.

Medical use of the minor tranquilizers is somewhat controversial. Their chief application is in the area of emotional (neurotic) problems. In our view, however, the more specific and more effective approach to the treatment of these problems is through individual or group psychotherapy. When those methods are used, the minor tranquilizers have a truly "minor" role to play. Their use is then restricted to those few instances when the patient is literally overwhelmed by anxiety. Lesser degrees of anxiety do not require drug treatment. In fact, psychological treatment cannot succeed when the patient is routinely provided with drug relief from his anxiety. Anxiety is the motor that powers psychological treatment. Anxiety together with other feelings is an indispensable guide to the progress of psychotherapy. When feelings are removed or impaired, as they invariably are with any psychoactive drug, the treatment itself is impaired. It is important for this type of psychiatric patient to understand this basis for the incompatibility between drug treatment and psychological treatment.

On the other hand, psychological approaches to treatment are sometimes unavailable. In such circumstances treatment with minor tranquilizers might be medically justifiable provided that the general medical and behavioral status of the patient is closely supervised. The physician must have at least enough understanding of the patient and his environment to assess, at any given time, whether or not the drug should be continued. The patient should always be realistically appraised of what can and cannot be expected from such use of a drug.

All of the intermediate depressants can also be abused. Their widespread medical use makes them available for abuse, but their slow onset of effects and the high doses necessary for euphoria tend to favor the barbiturates as agents of choice for abuse. Tolerance develops with the intermediate depressants, and the withdrawal syndrome seen with abrupt cessation of very high doses is similar in its features and its dangers to the withdrawal syndrome of barbiturates.

The major tranquilizers are a group of agents that are effective in diminishing the outward signs of psychosis. They are, for the most part, phenothiazines or phenothiazine derivatives. Chlorpromazine (Thorazine) is the most commonly used major tranquilizer, and it is very typical of this class of drugs. It is used basically for its quieting effect on psychotic patients. It reduces combativeness and increases relaxation and cooperativeness. The psychological action of chlorpromazine consists of an apparent indifference to external stimuli and the diminution of initiative and anxiety, with relatively little change in the state of waking or intellectual faculties. It tends to diminish spontaneous motor activity and may even give a cataleptic or "zombie" appearance. Chlorpromazine has no anti-convulsant effect, but it is a potent antiemetic (i.e., it prevents vomiting). Symptoms of psychosis, e.g., delusions and hallucinations, may be partially or completely suppressed by major tranquilizers. This is known as the anti-psychotic effect.

The reason the major tranquilizers are classed as special depressants is that, within a wide range of doses, they seem to depress bodily functions only to a certain point and no further. Chlorpromazine, for example, can be given in a dosage range from 25 mg per day to 5000 mg per day. Respiratory depression does not occur with high doses, and the ratio between a lethal dose and the minimum effective dose may be 250 to 1 or higher. The side effects of chlorpromazine include adverse neuromuscular reactions, jaundice, and skin reactions. The total incidence of all side effects is less than 3 percent.

The major tranquilizers are not addicting, as addiction is defined in this book. Neither craving nor compulsive abuse develops, perhaps because these agents do not produce euphoria. What may be a degree of physical dependence can occur (abrupt cessation can produce some restlessness and insomnia), but no well-defined withdrawal syndrome has been described. Although tolerance develops to the sedative effects, the anti-psychotic effects may endure throughout years of continuous treatment. During such prolonged treatment, however, periodic adjustment of the dosage is required.

The possibility of genetic and other chronic non-psychiatric hazards of phenothiazines is currently under investigation.[3] In any case the physician will have to weigh all the *possible* adverse effects against the very real behavioral improvement that these drugs can produce in psychotic states. In medical practice decisions must often be made in the face of many uncertainties.

Another group of special depressants consists of those agents found in non-prescription sleeping medications. Two main members of this group are scopolamine, a belladonna alkaloid, and methapyrilene (Histadyl), an antihistamine. These agents both produce a mild sedation with low doses, but they will not produce a deeper sedation with higher doses. They do not produce physical dependence or addiction, but tolerance does develop to their sedative effect. An important point to note about these two agents is that they are both quite toxic in high doses, especially to children, and should be treated with the same care as other dangerous medicines.

QUESTIONS

1. The chief use of the barbiturates is to produce sleep.
                    True or false? . . . . . .

2. Barbiturates can be used for the specific treatment of pain.
                    True or false? . . . . . .

3. The barbiturates have a greater "dependence liability" than do the other hypnotics.
                    True or false? . . . . . .

4. Withdrawal from the barbiturates is more dangerous than withdrawal from the narcotic analgesics.

True or false? ......

5. Barbiturates are often abused in conjunction with other drugs.

True or false? ......

6. Barbiturate overdose is a common cause of death.

True or false? ......

7. Driving under the influence of barbiturates or tranquilizers can be dangerous.

True or false? ......

8. The minor tranquilizers reduce feelings of anxiety and tension.

True or false? ......

9. The major tranquilizers reduce the symptoms of schizo-phrenia.

True or false? ......

ANSWERS

1. The chief use of the barbiturates is to produce sleep.

Answer: *True*. They are excellent for producing "sleep" or, more accurately, relief from insomnia. However, chronic use, especially when not medically supervised, may lead to the development of psychological dependence and tolerance. Tolerance necessitates higher doses, and higher doses increase the likelihood of both physical and psychological dependence.

2. Barbiturates can be used for the specific treatment of pain.

Answer: *False*. A frequent source of confusion here is the fact that some ultra-short acting barbiturates are used as general anesthetics (e.g., Sodium Pentothal). A general anesthetic is an agent that reduces the perception of all sensations, including pain, by the production of a state of unconsciousness. Analgesics, on the other hand, relieve pain without altering the state of consciousness. Barbiturates are anesthetics, but they are not effective as analgesics. Therefore, they should not be the primary medication for people suffering from pain.

3. The barbiturates have a greater "dependence liability" than do the other hypnotics.

Answer: *False*. There is no significant difference between the dependence liability of barbiturates and that of other hypnotics. The barbiturates are abused more than the other hypnotics because they are more available and less expensive. All the general depressants can and have been abused. Even the general anesthetics—ether and nitrous oxide, for example —have been abused.[4] Some intermediate depressants, how-

69

ever, seem to be abused less than the general depressants. The slow onset of action and the prolonged effect of chlordiazepoxide (Librium), for example, makes it less able to produce the typical general-depressant type of euphoria.

4. Withdrawal from the barbiturates is more dangerous than withdrawal from the narcotic analgesics.

Answer: *True*. Although withdrawal from the narcotic analgesics is quite unpleasant, it is not usually life-threatening. Withdrawal from the barbiturates, however, is not only unpleasant but can also be life-threatening. The dangers of barbiturate withdrawal are similar to the dangers of the delirium tremens syndrome.

5. Barbiturates are often abused in conjunction with other drugs.

Answer: *True*. Cases of dependence on barbiturates alone are not rare, but it is much commoner to find them abused in conjunction with other agents. Narcotic addicts will sometimes use barbiturates if narcotics are unavailable. Similarly, alcoholics will sometimes intoxicate themselves with barbiturates to avoid the smell of alcohol on their breath. A particularly vicious situation is the simultaneous abuse of barbiturates and amphetamines. This combination is sometimes called "ups and downs," and this combined abuse has many more disadvantages than the separate abuse of these agents. (See Chapter 4.)

6. Barbiturate overdose is a common cause of death.

Answer: *True*. Accidental barbiturate poisoning is common because of the low therapeutic ratio of these drugs and because the development of tolerance does not markedly elevate the lethal dose. Furthermore, barbiturates are commonly used in suicide attempts, a significant proportion of which are successful. From 1957 through 1963, 8,469 cases of barbiturate poisoning and 1,165 barbiturate fatalities were reported for New York City alone. One half of these were suicide attempts.[5]

7. Driving under the influence of barbiturates or tranquilizers can be dangerous.

Answer: *True.* The dangers of driving under the influence of barbiturates or tranquilizers are the same as the dangers of driving under the influence of alcohol. Judgment and co-ordination can be significantly impaired, and reaction time is slowed. A person being medicated with these drugs should not drive an automobile or operate machinery, unless it can be conclusively demonstrated that the drugs do not affect him in this way. Even then, the utmost caution should be exercised. Furthermore, the effect of alcohol upon someone taking these medications is significantly enhanced. A person whose driving is not impaired by a given dose of alcohol may suffer signif-icant deterioration of performance if he uses that same dose of alcohol and also takes a barbiturate or tranquilizer.

8. The minor tranquilizers reduce feelings of anxiety and tension.

Answer: *True.* The minor tranquilizers reduce feelings of anxiety and tension, but it must be emphasized that they are not curative agents. They act to relieve these symptoms of a deeper disorder or disturbance, but they do nothing to affect the cause of the problems. Drug treatment by itself is of little value in the overall treatment of emotional problems. Such problems are handled best with individual or group psycho-logical techniques. Individualization of treatment by psycho-logical techniques can provide more specific help for emotional (neurotic) problems than is possible with any drug. In such cases use of the minor tranquilizers is limited to the management of extreme anxiety that would otherwise incapacitate the patient.

9. The major tranquilizers reduce the symptoms of schizophrenia.

Answer: *True*. The major tranquilizers diminish the outward signs of psychosis, but it is not yet known whether they affect the disturbance itself. The value of this effect is not to be minimized, however. The use of major tranquilizers in treating psychotic patients has helped thousands of people, who might otherwise have spent most of their lives in mental institutions, make satisfactory adjustments to society.[6]

CASE 3-1

A fifteen year-old young man is brought to see you. He is a junior in an inner-city high school and was found unconscious at his desk in study hall. Barbiturate capsules were found in his pocket. The principal of the school and the guidance counselors have sought your advice on how to deal with this boy's problem.

He is an intelligent, alert, and personable adolescent, who is neither hostile nor uncommunicative. When you ask him to tell you what led to his "passing out" in school, he answers willingly. He has been taking "goofballs" for two years, he says. He takes them to "loosen up," especially at parties and other social gatherings. He likes to dance, and he says "pills" help him overcome his inhibitions about being the "life of the party," a role he carefully cultivates. He prefers the barbiturates to wine, which he occasionally uses for the same purpose, because the barbiturates don't make him sick or give him a hangover.

When you ask him why he is taking "pills" at school, he replies he doesn't do it very often, just once or twice a week. He says that it's because school has been boring him lately and that with "pills" he doesn't care about his boredom. He could drink wine, he says, but "pills" don't make his breath smell and nobody can tell he's high.

He tells you he has taken heroin twice and liked it, but says he doesn't plan to use heroin again because he doesn't want to get addicted. Finally, he asks you if "pills" are dangerous.

In this situation what would you do?

(A) Tell him "pills" are dangerous and that if he doesn't stop taking them he may become addicted or die of an overdose.

(B) Ask him whether he thinks "pills" are dangerous.

(C) Suggest the following (write your own solution):

. . . .

. . . .

. . . .

. . . .

. . . .

DISCUSSION

This young man's question—are "pills" dangerous?—has a deeper meaning. It is a test that will determine how he will react to anything you tell him. An authoritarian response, such as choice (A), telling him that "pills" are dangerous and that if he doesn't stop taking them he may become addicted or die of an overdose, although true, may create a great deal of resistance in him. You need to develop a feeling of trust with this adolescent, if you are to have any helpful influence on him. You may not be able to do this if you make authoritarian statements before you have understood more about his situation.

Therefore, asking him whether he thinks "pills" are dangerous (B) is the proper response to his question. He probably does think they are dangerous, and his "passing out" in school has probably frightened him a great deal. Moreover, when dealing with people, and especially with young people, *how* something is said is often more important than *what* is actually said. If you reply to his question with another question, you give him the opportunity to express his fears in a less threatening fashion. Once these fears are expressed, a relationship may be established where you can work together toward a resolution of his problems. Alternative (A), however, will put this young man on the defensive and will cause him to deny or suppress his fears in order to respond to the challenge implicit in your statement. In such a situation, you will become adversaries rather than partners, and you will both be frustrated.

Assuming that you made a proper choice and that this young

man has expressed his fears about the drugs but has also said that he is not sure he will stop taking them, what would you tell his school principal and guidance counselors?

(A) Tell them that this young man is mentally ill and needs hospitalization for his drug problem.

(B) Tell them that this young man is basically stable and that with proper direction and counseling he will get over his drug problem.

(C) Suggest the following (write your own suggestion):

. . . .

. . . .

. . . .

. . . .

. . . .

DISCUSSION

At this time, neither of the two choices offered above would be appropriate, even though one of them may be correct in fact. The important point is that you do not have enough information to ascertain whether this young man is seriously disturbed or not. He may be suffering from the insecurity, self-consciousness, and uncertainty of adolescence, and be responding to these feelings in a fashion that is common in his environment. He may need only redirection and encouragement. On the other hand, his central problem may involve a very disturbed child-parent relationship. As long as no attention is given to the home situation, redirection at school may accomplish nothing.

Speculation, it should be remembered, is no substitute for information. It is imperative to explore the background and setting of people's problems. Unless this is done in every case, the chance of having any helpful effect is greatly reduced.

CASE 3-2

A twenty-five year-old man comes to you for "medical advice." He is an auto mechanic who lives alone. He has a long history of psychiatric illness and has been hospitalized several times for acute psychotic episodes, diagnosed as schizophrenia. At the present time, however, his symptoms are well controlled by phenothiazine medication dispensed by the state mental hospital in the city. He also participates in group therapy twice a month at this hospital, but he feels that they really don't pay much attention to him there. The hospital is overcrowded and understaffed, and actually can do very little for its outpatients other than providing them with medication.

The reason he has come to see you is that some of his relatives think that he should not be taking so many tranquilizers all of the time because he isn't sick right now. They are afraid he will become addicted to them. He says he was told by the doctors at the hospital that he would have to take these pills for the rest of his life. He says he wants to follow the doctor's orders, but he doesn't want to become an addict.

If you were the doctor, what would you do?

- (A) Reassure him that the tranquilizers he is taking are not addicting and that he need not worry about becoming a drug addict.
- (B) Suggest that since he is having no problems at the present time, he stop taking the tranquilizers.
- (C) Tell him he worries too much.
- (D) Suggest the following (write your own solution):

. . . .

. . . .

. . . .

. . . .

. . . .

DISCUSSION

Suggesting that, since he is having no problems at the present time, he stop taking the tranquilizers (B), is probably not the best choice here. Although approximately one-third of schizophrenic patients can stop using these medications without a recurrence of symptoms, there is no way to predict when drug treatment can be safely discontinued.[7] It is necessary to interrupt the drug treatment and observe the results. Symptoms may take as long as six months to develop; therefore, withdrawal should proceed slowly and under close psychiatric supervision. Consultation with the previous physician or reference to hospital records can provide a valuable guide to the patient's past reactions to medication as well as to his pattern of relapse.

Telling him he worries too much (C) is a form of denial on your part. You may be very busy, but the few minutes you take to reassure him that the tranquilizers he is taking are not addicting and that he need not worry about becoming an addict (A) may well save him from much future misery. You should explain to this man that some medicines, even when taken every day, are not necessarily addicting. You might mention that some diabetics have to take insulin every day but are not addicted to it. This man is worried about the possibility of becoming addicted to phenothiazines. In this situation it is important to understand the definition of addiction (see Chapter 1). It is also important to explain the difference between regular use of a drug for control of illness and the pattern of compulsive abuse of increasingly larger and larger amounts of a drug for cyclical, self-induced changes in mood.

CASE 3-3

A twenty-five year-old woman comes to see you. She is a housewife with two small children, aged one and three. Both she and her husband are college graduates. She majored in English literature, and he is an engineer. They married right after graduation. He is working for a small electronics firm, of which he is part owner; she has not worked at all. Because of the size of the company and the competitiveness of the industry, it is necessary for her husband to work long hours to ensure the success of the venture. He tells his wife that it won't always be like this, but that until the company is firmly established it will take hard work and sacrifice from both of them. She understands the situation and wants to do nothing to stand in her husband's way. However, this means she is "cooped up" in the house all day with the two babies. It's not that she doesn't love them, she says, it's just that housework, diapers, and crying babies get on her nerves. Sometimes she gets so worked up, she says, she feels like screaming. She would like to get out of the house, but the children are too young for nursery school, and her parents and in-laws live too far away to help take care of them.

She says that when she's nervous she finds herself shouting at the children and snapping at her husband, and this makes her even more upset. She asks you to give her something to "calm her nerves," so she can cope with her situation without taking her frustrations and nervousness out on her children and her husband.

If you were her doctor, what would you do?

(A) Give the woman a prescription for tranquilizers.

(B) Give the woman a placebo. (A placebo is an inert or

harmless medication—a "sugar pill"—given to patients to satisfy their desire for medication.)

(C) Give the woman no medication, but instead try to find out more about her and her husband, and arrange to discuss at greater length the source of her problems and the various possible means of coping with them.

(D) Suggest the following (write your own solution):

. . . .

. . . .

. . . .

. . . .

. . . .

DISCUSSION

This is one of the most significant cases in this book. In theory, one of the choices is better than the others. But when a physician is confronted with this situation in his office (and situations like this can account for 10 to 50 percent of a physician's patient load), all three choices have grave drawbacks.

By now, you should have been able to figure out, or to at least guess, that giving this woman tranquilizers (A) is not the best choice in this situation. There are many reasons for this. One is that you would be treating the manifestations of her problem, but not the real problem. Besides, even this symptomatic relief is not free of hazards. Tolerance develops to the effects of the minor tranquilizers (the major tranquilizers should not be considered in this situation); and after a time, this woman would probably have a recurrence of her "nervousness," which would require either an increased dosage, a switch to a different medication, or both. A drug dependence could be established in this woman as a result of one initially harmless and well-intentioned prescription for a minor tranquilizer.

A further danger of prescribing a tranquilizer is the possibility of an idiosyncratic allergic or toxic reaction. However, such reactions that may involve the skin, bone marrow, nervous system or other organs can occur almost any time any drug (penicillin, for instance) is given, and reactions cannot be predicted on the basis of the existence (or lack of it) of an allergy to any other substance. Although the incidence of idiosyncratic reactions is low and fatalities are rare, they do occur. A person who is suffering from a drug reaction is not reassured by the fact that such reactions are uncommon.

But then, would not a placebo (B) solve these problems? Yes, it would initially eliminate the possibility of physical dependence or drug reaction. But there are many complications involved in this choice. Do not underestimate the placebo. Although it has no direct physical or chemical effect on the brain or the body, it has a powerful effect on the mind— the power of suggestion, the same power used by a "faith healer." Most ill or troubled people will feel better just from being seen and reassured by a physician. Many people, when told by a physician, "Take this medicine, and you'll feel better soon," *will* feel better soon, regardless of what the medicine actually is. This is not hocus-pocus or quackery. The power of suggestion and the placebo are very important therapeutic tools that have their rightful place in the proper practice of medicine (and in other fields as well).

However, any powerful tool has disadvantages. A chief one here is discovery by the patient. If you give this woman a placebo and some reassurance, perhaps she would feel better and never need other medication for her "nerves" again. But this is an unlikely possibility. It is more likely that she will come back and ask for something stronger. However, even if she never requested another medication, there would still be a disadvantage. In responding to this woman's emotional needs with a *medication,* no matter how innocuous, you have reinforced a common behavioral pattern. In our society, the prevailing mode of coping with discomfort of all sorts is pharmacological. We take aspirin for headaches, antacids for upset stomach, "cold tablets" for colds, sleeping pills for insomnia, vitamins and tonics for "tired blood," and tranquilizers for emotional problems. We have trained ourselves to reach into the medicine cabinet to cure everything from dandruff to tired feet. Physicians have contributed to this by abusing the power of the placebo—by prescribing unnecessary or even inappropriate medicine for their patients. Millions in our society, including patients and their physicians, have fallen victim to the fantasy that miracles can be found in bottles. This may be a drug-oriented society, but if this woman reaches for a pill whenever she gets upset, what will she say to her children when they get older and perhaps imitate her behavior, except with different pills?

This leaves choice (C). Talking more with this woman to find out more about her and her husband and discussing, at length, various possible means of coping with her problems is the best choice. This may not be easy, however, and for some physicians it may not be possible. Many physicians do not have the training to undertake such a role. And most physicians, regardless of their training, do not have the *time* needed for this counseling role. Furthermore, many patients would not be satisfied with such a response. Many patients go to see a physician to get medicine so they will feel better. If one physician will not give them this medicine, they will go to another and another, in a seemingly endless search for the "right doctor and the right medicine." Finally, it is easy to underestimate the pressure felt by a physician in this situation. A physician has had from nine to more than twelve years of education and training beyond a high-school diploma. He spends all this time, plus all the time he is in practice, in order to help people. He learns that there are some medications that can postpone death and alleviate suffering. He feels great satisfaction when he can help a sick person, and great frustration and inadequacy when he cannot. A busy physician, when confronted with a situation like this, often feels that he really cannot take the time to help this woman solve her problems and still fulfill his professional responsibilities to his other patients. Knowing this, and yet wanting to help this woman, he may prescribe a medication, not only to make her feel better (if only temporarily) but also to make himself feel better.

Probably the best course of action for the physician would

be to refer this woman to the agency or counselor who can take the time required to help her work out her personal problems without drugs. But even this course is not free from possible drawbacks. Many people, as mentioned above, come to physicians for the sole purpose of receiving a medication for their "illness." Often these people will not accept such a referral, and will interpret it as a sign of rejection by their physician. It may require more time to persuade such patients to seek the referral than it would to resolve a similar problem in another type of patient.

The problem, it should be emphasized, is not unsolvable. A talented counselor—whether he is a physician, social worker, psychologist, or clergyman—should be able to help this family. But this case illustrates some of the difficulties and barriers that may obstruct a successful resolution to such problems.

Many implications of this case relate directly to the complexities of the so-called drug problem. It is a sad fact of life that, as in this situation, good people often harm each other, not out of malice, but with the best will in the world. The "drug problem" is actually only millions of individual "people problems." All the problems are different, but all are somehow the same.

NOTES

1. S. K. Sharpless, "Hypnotics and Sedatives," in *The Pharmacological Basis of Therapeutics,* 4th edition, ed. L. S. Goodman and A. Gilman (New York: Macmillan Company, 1970), p. 115.

2. H. F. Fraser *et al.,* "Degree of Physical Dependence Induced by Secobarbital or Phenobarbital," *Journal of the American Medical Association* 166, no. 2 (11 January 1958): p. 128.

3. P. S. Moorehead, L. F. Jarvik, and M. M. Cohen, "Cytogenetic Methods for Mutagenicity Testing," in S. S. Epstein, ed., *Drugs of Abuse: Their Genetic and Other Chronic Non-Psychiatric Hazards,* (Cambridge, Massachusetts: M.I.T. Press, 1971), p. 152.

4. J. F. Jaffe, "Drug Addiction and Drug Abuse," in *The Pharmacological Basis of Therapeutics,* 4th edition, p. 300.

5. Sharpless, "Hypnotics and Sedatives," p. 115.

6. M. E. Jarvik, "Drugs Used in the Treatment of Psychiatric Disorders," in *The Pharmacological Basis of Therapeutics,* 4th edition, p. 167.

7. *Ibid.,* p. 168.

Chapter 4

AMPHETAMINES
AND COCAINE

The amphetamines and cocaine are the most commonly used stimulant drugs. The term amphetamines refers not only to amphetamine itself (Benzedrine, Dexedrine) but also to certain related drugs, such as methamphetamine (Methedrine). The amphetamines are members of a class of drugs that are called sympathomimetic amines because their effects tend to mimic the action of the sympathetic nervous system (SNS). The SNS is particularly active in states of arousal—such as fear, rage, and anxiety—and is responsible for the tachycardia (increase in heart rate), tachypnea (increase in respiratory rate), sweating, mydriasis (dilation of the pupils), tremor, and hypertension (increase in blood pressure) that are so noticeable at these times. The sympathomimetic amines all have these effects, but the amphetamines also have the effect of increasing a person's sense of well-being. They are "mood elevators." They induce a feeling of wakefulness and alertness, decrease the sense of fatigue, cause loss of appetite. They increase confidence and they induce elation and euphoria. This elevation of mood is the principal reason for the abuse of amphetamines. In the amphetamine abuser drug-induced increase in activity can lead to violence.[1]

In 1962, 100,000 pounds of amphetamines were produced,

or about 10 billion 5 mg doses (5 mg is the minimum effective dose).[2] The most common use of these agents has been in "diet pills." Since amphetamines cause a depression of appetite, their use may lead to a decrease in food intake and weight loss. However, since tolerance to this effect of the amphetamines develops rapidly, amphetamines are ineffective in the long run for treatment of obesity. Other medical uses of amphetamines include the treatment of people with narcolepsy (a disease characterized by abrupt, involuntary onset of sleep) and of certain hyperactive children who suffer from neuropsychiatric disturbances called "minimal brain dysfunction." (Amphetamines, paradoxically, have a calming effect upon these children.)

As stimulants they are thought to be antidotes to the depressant drugs, but pharmacologically this is not so. For example, the adverse effect of barbiturates on paradoxical sleep (see Chapter 3) is actually worsened when an amphetamine is added.

Amphetamines are frequently abused in combination with barbiturates or alcohol. Sometimes they are used by narcotic addicts when heroin is unavailable. Amphetamines can be administered either orally or intravenously, and the effect of a single dose lasts several hours.

Most people begin abusing amphetamines orally. Tolerance quickly develops to the mood-elevating effects of initial doses in the range of 10–20 mg. The compulsive user may consequently increase his daily intake to 250–1000 mg per day. However, once daily intake reaches 150–250 mg, the compulsive user commonly begins to administer the drug intravenously in doses that may result in a daily intake of 5000 mg per day.[3] "Graduation to the needle" may result from persuasion by other users that the "high" is better. The intravenous user experiences the "rush" which is sought after as an orgasmic release of tension.

The intravenous use of amphetamines is very dangerous. It involves all of the complications of needle contamination (serum hepatitis, endocarditis, and other kinds of infection) that were mentioned in the discussion of the narcotic analgesics, as well as a toxic psychosis directly due to high doses of the drug. The toxic psychosis associated with the use of large doses of amphetamines involves vivid auditory and visual hallucinations, paranoid thinking, an inability to see relationships, a loosening of associations, and changes in emotional responses. The senses, however, remain clear; there is no blurring of vision, for example. The toxic psychosis caused by amphetamines may be difficult to differentiate from a schizophrenic reaction. However, the toxic psychosis will usually clear spontaneously within one week after cessation of the use of amphetamines. Although tolerance develops to most effects of the amphetamines—for example, chronic users may have no elevation of blood pressure, or of heart or respiratory rate—no tolerance develops to the toxic effects of the amphetamines on the brain, i.e., the toxic psychosis. This behavioral toxicity seems related to the dose and chronicity of use.

Abrupt cessation of high-dosage amphetamine use produces no classical withdrawal syndrome. The only physical signs of withdrawal are some changes on the electroencephalogram (EEG). These may be indicative of some form of physical dependence. However, withdrawal produces marked psychological changes, including marked craving for the drug, overwhelming fatigue, lassitude, and a depression so severe it may provoke suicide. In response to these feelings of depression and fatigue, the amphetamine abuser will usually begin another cycle of repetitive, compulsive use.

The toxic single dose of an amphetamine varies with the individual. In those persons who have not developed tolerance, it may be as little as 30 mg. The effects of a toxic nonfatal dose include confusion, assaultiveness, and anxiety; and the effects may progress to hallucinations and panic states, marked by suicidal or homicidal tendencies, especially in unstable persons. Death has been recorded in non-tolerant individuals from a dose of 120 mg, yet a single dose of 500 mg has been survived. The cause of death in acute cases is usually cerebral hemorrhage. The toxic single dose in tolerant individuals can be much higher; but again, the toxic dose varies among individuals.

Another commonly abused stimulant, cocaine, is a natural derivative of the coca leaf. The coca plant (not to be confused with the kola plant or the cacao plant both of which produce caffeine) grows in Peru where the Indian natives chew its leaves. The cocaine in the leaves has a local anesthetic effect on the mouth, and it also acts as a central nervous system stimulant. The effects of pure cocaine are very similar to those of the amphetamines, except that the duration of the effects is only from a few minutes to a half hour. Amphetamines show cross tolerance among themselves but not with cocaine. It is not certain whether tolerance develops to the effects of cocaine.[4] Like the amphetamines, the use of cocaine is associated with a toxic psychosis; and although craving and depression may be severe, withdrawal produces no overt physical symptoms. The subjective effects of cocaine are so similar to those of the amphetamines that even experienced users may not at first be able to distinguish between the two; furthermore, amphetamine addicts describe the effects of their drug in almost the same terms cocaine addicts use.

Cocaine may be sniffed ("snorted") as a powder ("snow") or injected intravenously, either alone or in combination with heroin. The latter combination is known as a "speedball" and is the most common form of cocaine use. Pure cocaine addiction is rare in the United States. Large-scale abuse of cocaine is a sporadic phenomenon in comparison with the more steady abuse of amphetamines. This can be explained by the greater difficulty of obtaining cocaine. Amphetamines, on the other hand, are often synthesized within the country by illicit laboratories.

QUESTIONS

1. Amphetamines can improve the motor performance of athletes.

   True or false? ......

2. Diet pills containing amphetamines act mainly by increasing the rate at which the body burns food.

   True or false? ......

3. Diet pills containing amphetamines will not help a compulsive eater lose weight.

   True or false? ......

4. High doses of amphetamines can lead to violent behavior.

   True or false? ......

5. Amphetamines will reverse the effects of low doses of barbiturates.

   True or false? ......

6. A person must have a personality disturbance in order to feel euphoria from amphetamines.

   True or false? ......

7. The amphetamines, as a group, display cross-tolerance.

   True or false? ......

8. The reason amphetamines are used more than cocaine is

because of the pleasanter drug effect achieved with amphetamines.

True or false? . . . . . .

9. There is no legitimate medical use for cocaine.

True or false? . . . . . .

10. The intravenous injection of amphetamines or cocaine produces a "rush."

True or false? . . . . . .

11. Prolonged use of the amphetamines may be physically harmful.

True or false? . . . . . .

ANSWERS

1. Amphetamines can improve the motor performance of athletes.

Answer: *True.* Amphetamines do not improve the intrinsic performance of athletes but act by a reduction of the feelings of fatigue. This effect is most prominent in endurance sports, such as long-distance running and bicycle racing. This can become dangerous and even deadly if, under the influence of the drug, the body is pushed past safe limits of endurance to total exhaustion. Normal fatigue provides a person with vital feedback of information about his body. To ignore this truth in the name of sport is both cynical and brutal.

2. Diet pills containing amphetamines act mainly by increasing the rate at which the body burns food.

Answer: *False.* Amphetamines may increase the rate at which the body burns food, but this increase is not enough to account for the weight loss that sometimes is seen with diet pills. The weight loss seen with amphtamines is due to a suppression of the appetite and a consequent decrease in food intake. However, tolerance to this effect develops within a few weeks.

3. Diet pills containing amphetamines will not help a compulsive eater lose weight.

Answer: *True.* A compulsive eater is a person whose eating is a symptom of psychophysiological problems. Such a person might be called a food addict. These people tend to eat in response to signals from their emotions and not to signals from their appetite. Therefore, amphetamines and appetite suppression do not help them lose weight.

4. High doses of amphetamines can lead to violent behavior.

Answer: *True*. Of all the drugs considered in this book, the amphetamines and cocaine are the most likely to lead to violent behavior. Many crimes of violence have been associated with the use of these agents. This effect of the amphetamines is particularly pronounced and dangerous in unstable or potentially unstable people.[5]

5. Amphetamines will reverse the effects of low doses of barbiturates.

Answer: *True*. Amphetamines will easily reverse the effects of a hypnotic dose of barbiturates and will counteract the respiratory depression due to these agents. However, the use of amphetamines to stimulate respiration in depressant drug poisoning, such as barbiturate overdose, is questionable. A mild case of poisoning will not require these agents; and in a severe case, the use of amphetamines can lead to a very unstable heart rate, respiratory rate, and blood pressure. Cases of drug overdose should always be treated by a physician and, whenever possible, in a hospital. "Home remedies" are totally inappropriate in these medical emergencies.

6. A person must have a personality disturbance in order to feel euphoria from amphetamines.

Answer: *False*. Every person will feel an increased sense of well-being from amphetamines. However, those with a deep need for such chemically induced feelings of well-being are much more likely to become involved in the compulsive abuse of amphetamines than are people with better integrated personalities.

7. The amphetamines, as a group, display cross-tolerance.

Answer: *True*. Tolerance to the amphetamines is believed to result, at least in part, from a depletion of the store of norepinephrine in the brain. As this store becomes more and more depleted, it requires increasingly larger amounts of amphetamines to release the little remaining norepinephrine. Since all of the amphetamines have this same releasing effect, tolerance to one member of the group produces tolerance to all members. Tolerance to the amphetamines *is* accompanied by a marked elevation of the lethal dose.

8. The reason amphetamines are used more than cocaine is because of the pleasanter drug effect achieved with amphetamines.

Answer: *False*. The reason amphetamines are used more than cocaine is probably because they are more readily available and are cheaper. The initial drug effect of the amphetamines and cocaine is almost identical, but the effect of amphetamines lasts several times as long as that of cocaine. Tolerance, however, does not seem to occur with cocaine.

9. There is no legitimate medical use for cocaine.

Answer: *False*. Cocaine was originally used medically as a local anesthetic. It is still occasionally used for that purpose. Synthetics have been produced, such as procaine (Novocain) and lidocaine (Xylocaine), that have the same local anesthetic properties as cocaine but that do not have a stimulating effect on the CNS and are not addicting. These synthetic local anesthetics have, for the most part, supplanted the use of cocaine in medicine.

10. The intravenous injection of amphetamines or cocaine produces a "rush."

Answer: *True*. The "rush" produced by intravenous injection of amphetamines or cocaine is described as being somewhat different from the "rush" produced by intravenous injection of narcotics, but still very pleasurable. Although tolerance rapidly develops to almost every other effect of the amphetamines, it does not seem to develop as rapidly to the "rush." Intravenous amphetamine addicts who have developed very high tolerances will often inject themselves every fifteen to twenty minutes for several days at a time, not so much for the stimulant effects, but rather for the "rush."

11. Prolonged use of the amphetamines may be physically harmful.

Answer: *True*. Although occasional use of the amphetamines may not be physiologically harmful, even small doses may, depending on the individual, lead to violent or antisocial behavior. This, of course, depends on the dose, the individual, and the motivation for the use of the drug. Prolonged use of large doses of amphetamines is very dangerous. A common phrase heard in the discussion of amphetamines is "speed kills." The chief causes of death among amphetamine addicts are marked malnutrition and debilitation due to lack of food, lack of sleep, and inadequate personal hygiene; hepatitis and infection, due to needle contamination; and violence. A recent study also reported that a disease of the blood vessels called necrotizing angiitis may be a cause of death in some addicts who take amphetamines intravenously.[6]

CASE 4-1

A nineteen year-old college sophomore comes to see you. It is near the end of the semester, and he tells you that he's behind in all of his courses, has two papers to write, and three finals to take. He says he doesn't know how he can do all his work and pass his courses. This semester, he tells you, he became very involved with a girl and also with extracurricular obligations; and between these two demands on his time, he was unable to do enough studying.

The reason he has come to see you, he says, is that his fraternity brother has some amphetamines and offered to sell him some to help him finish his work. He says that he's never taken any pills before, just smoked some marihuana once, and that he has heard the expression "speed kills." He wonders what to do. He has to do something to finish his work, but he is afraid the drugs may harm him some way.

In this situation, what would you tell him?

(A) That under no circumstances should he take the amphetamines.

(B) That if he takes the amphetamines, he is likely to suffer both physical and psychological harm.

(C) That taking a few amphetamine pills probably won't hurt him physically, but that they probably won't help his academic performance either.

(D) That it's all right to take an amphetamine now and then.

(E) Suggest the following (write your own solution):

. . . .

. . . .

. . . .

. . . .

. . . .

DISCUSSION

Telling this young man that under no circumstances should he take the amphetamines (A) is as unwise as telling him it's all right to take them now and then (D). Both of these responses are, in a sense, telling him what to do. What he needs from you at this point, however, is not advice, but rather accurate and appropriate information to enable him to make the right decision for himself by himself. If you give him advice, even proper advice, you may help him with his present problem, but you will not have helped him develop mature decision-making abilities that he will need in facing future choices and problems.

For these reasons, telling him that he is likely to suffer both physical and psychological harm from taking the amphetamines (B) is also doing him an injustice. Although there is a finite risk of physical and psychological harm in any self-administration of amphetamines (and most other drugs as well), these risks must be placed in their proper perspective. The risks are much greater in compulsive intravenous use than they are in intermittent oral use for the purpose of staying awake. Telling him (B) is only giving him part of the "facts," as we know them. It is too close to scare tactics to be effective. Furthermore, if he disregards your warnings, takes the amphetamines, and feels that he has not suffered any harm, he will no longer seek your advice nor believe almost anything else you say about drugs, no matter how accurate.

Therefore, telling him that taking a few amphetamine pills probably won't hurt him physically, but probably will not help his academic performance either (C), is a reasonable choice. Although this may seem permissive, and even encouraging, it is accurate. In this situation, this college student may take the amphetamines out of desperation, regardless of what you say. But if you provide him with accurate information, he will have a better foundation upon which to base his decision. He will also have the experience of suffering the consequences of a decision that was made with knowledge of the possible outcomes. Furthermore, he will tend to trust you in your future dealings with him.

On the other hand this student may be literally asking for outside help to control his urge to do something that he already regards as potentially self-destructive. The catalog of his activities and "involvements" suggests that he may feel overwhelmed now that finals are to be added to his burden. If he has already decided to use the drug, why has he bothered to see you at all? If he really wants you to say "no" will his feeling of control be further undermined by your relatively non-committal attitude? Perhaps it would be appropriate to inquire further into his ideas about amphetamines and their effects. The feelings that he displays while talking may be as important or more important than what he says. Sensitivity to such feelings might lead to confirmation of the counselor's idea that the student's real motive is to bolster his feeling of control. If that turns out to be so, discussion of various personal aspects of control over his behavior will take precedence over a narrow dialog about the drug, but the drug could still be factually discussed in the manner outlined above. This case is an important and a very typical example of a situation where the presenting problem may only be a prelude to a more general and a more important psychological problem. It should also be noted that working on a psychological level is very appropriate in a case that is devoid of the pharmacological consequences of drug dependence. Elsewhere in this book, it will be shown that where such complications occur, they must be dealt with in their entirety before the psychological approach can be effective.

CASE 4-2

A nineteen year-old secretary comes to see you. She is quite obese, and her chart shows that she is 5'3" tall and weighs 195 pounds. She asks you to give her some "diet pills," so she can lose weight. During the conversation, she tells you she has always been chubby. She was an only child and remembers her childhood as being unhappy. Her parents did not get along, and she had few friends. Most of the children would tease her about being fat. Her only consolation was food. Whenever she felt bad, her mother would give her something to eat. She says that even now she eats whenever she gets depressed and that this happens all the time. When you ask her why she is depressed, she says it's because she's so fat. She says that no one likes her, that she doesn't have any friends, and that she never gets asked out on dates. It's a vicious circle because the only way she can make herself feel better is to eat something, which only makes her fatter and uglier and more depressed. She has tried all kinds of diets, she says, but never found one that worked for her. She has never taken "diet pills" before, but now she is getting desperate.

If you were the doctor, what would you do?

(A) Give her a prescription for amphetamines and a low-calorie diet program to follow.
(B) Refer her to a group weight-reduction program, such as "Weight-Watchers."
(C) Refer her for psychological evaluation and therapy.
(D) Suggest the following (write your own solution):

. . . .

. . . .

. . . .

. . . .

. . . .

DISCUSSION

The most obvious thing you can say about this case is that giving this young woman amphetamines (A) is very unwise. She is an example of what can be called, although it is unscientific, a food addict. She eats as a pathological response to feelings of depression and inferiority. This condition bears some resemblance to alcoholism, but, of course, it does not involve any intoxication. Like many true addictions, this type of overeating does involve an inappropriate response to the pressures of daily living and to feelings of personal inadequacy. Both conditions may lead to serious organic disease in the long run. Giving her amphetamines to help her stop eating would be similar to giving an alcoholic barbiturates to help him stop drinking.

This young woman has some insight into her basic problems, and she sincerely wants to do something about them. A group weight-reduction program, such as "Weight-Watchers" (B), might be very helpful in this case. Such programs operate on the principles of mutual support and group goals and responsibilities. They are operationally similar to Alcoholics Anonymous; and such programs can be very beneficial for those who want to help themselves. However, they are clearly not for everyone.

Referring her for psychological evaluation and therapy (C) is also a good choice. She wants help, and it should not be too difficult to persuade her to seek it from the proper sources. In any case, however, the task is the same. She has to acquire a new life style. This is a major task for any person, and it requires a great deal of motivation and persistence. These factors are much more important than is the route she chooses to accomplish this change. All such programs, when properly utilized, can be extremely effective. But the person must have the desire and the will to overcome his problem.

It must be acknowledged that the basic causes of obesity are unknown. Research on certain appetite-regulating centers in the brain may lead to greater understanding of the mechanisms of weight control.

CASE 4-3

A fifteen year-old boy is brought to see you. He was caught shoplifting in a department store and was turned over to juvenile authorities. He is a runaway and had been missing for five months. He is thin and malnourished, and he has many sores on his face and arms.

He is hostile and uncommunicative at first; but after some small talk and gently probing questions, he begins to tell his story. He says he ran away because his parents fought all the time and didn't understand him. He was not very involved with drugs at home, but he was introduced to "speed" soon after he ran away. During those five months, he took any kind of pill he could get his hands on, but preferred amphetamines. He is afraid of needles, so he never "shot" speed, he says, but only "dropped" (orally ingested) it. He reports that he would scrounge, steal, or beg for food and money for drugs. When you ask him if he would like to continue living in that way, he replies, "No, I guess not. It's too much of a hassle." But he also says that he would rather be on the street than go back home and that he will just run away again if you try to make him go home. His parents have been notified of their son's situation and are trying to make arrangements to have him returned to them. The ultimate disposition of this case depends in large part upon the recommendations you make.

In this situation what would you do?

(A) Recommend that he be returned to the custody of his parents.
(B) Recommend that he be hospitalized for rehabilitation.

(C) Recommend that he be placed in a foster home.
(D) Recommend that he be placed in a reform school.
(E) Recommend that he be hospitalized for rehabilitation and that the parents seek counseling for the entire family.
(F) Suggest the following (write your own solution):

. . . .

. . . .

. . . .

. . . .

. . . .

DISCUSSION

Recommending that this boy be returned to the custody of his parents (A) is an invitation to disaster. It is in no way therapeutic and will probably lead to another runaway, with perhaps even more severe consequences.

Recommending that he be placed in a reform school (D) is also inappropriate. This boy is not a hardened criminal; he is seriously disturbed. He needs psychological therapy and rehabilitation. For this reason, placing him in a foster home (C) is not the best choice. Although the change in environment would probably be helpful, it is not enough by itself. Similarly, hospitalizing him for rehabilitation (B) is not enough either. What is necessary is hospitalization for rehabilitation *and* family counseling (E). This approach responds to this boy's immediate and pressing need for therapy and rehabilitation and also attempts to resolve the basic conflicts that led to his running away and his drug use. Such an approach does not guarantee success, but anything less is surely doomed to failure.

CASE 4-4

You are asked to comment on the prospects of rehabilitating a twenty-one year-old man who was taken into custody during a public disturbance when he was in a highly agitated and psychotic state.

He speaks quite willingly about himself and especially about his drug experiences. He has been using various kinds of drugs since he was eighteen, but he first began taking amphetamines two years ago. He found the key to himself in "speed," he says. It "opened his mind" and gave him a feeling of power and confidence in himself that he had never felt before. He couldn't resist this feeling and soon was "dropping" several hundred milligrams a day. He became involved with a crowd that was shooting "crystal" (pure crystalline methamphetamine), and about a year ago he started "shooting speed" himself. He describes his pattern of drug use as alternating "runs" and "crashes." He would start a "run," "shooting" every few hours, at first, until he was "really flying." This would continue for several days. As the run progressed, he would "shoot" more and more often; not so much for the stimulant effect of the drug, but more for the "fantastic rush" it would give him. During the "run," he would write and talk and keep busy for hours on end. He wouldn't sleep at all; and although he would try to force himself to eat intermittently, he would actually eat very little. After about five to seven days on a "run," he would begin to get "freaky." He would get very paranoid and would always be getting into arguments and sometimes even fights. Although he would "shoot" more and more often, the "rushes" would diminish in intensity, and he would be so paranoid and disorganized he

109

couldn't even take any more drug. At this point he would "crash," either by spontaneously falling asleep or by taking some barbiturates to do so. He would sleep from eighteen to as long as thirty-six hours, depending on the length of the "run," and would awaken totally exhausted and depressed. He would try to eat whatever he could get his hands on; but he would feel so lethargic during a "crash" that he felt he would either have to commit suicide or take some more drug for a lift, and thus begin another "run."

He has been fed and cared for in the six weeks since his arrest, but he still looks malnourished and chronically ill. He is over most of the depression and lethargy of his last "crash." When you ask him what he plans on doing when he is released, he says, "I just don't know. Speed will probably kill me, but I don't know if I can resist it."

In this situation what would you do?

(A) Have him committed to an institution, either voluntarily or not (if necessary), for long-term psychotherapy and rehabilitation.

(B) Have him released when he has physically recovered, on the condition that he not use amphetamines and seek psychotherapy.

(C) Have him released when he has physically recovered.

(D) Suggest the following (write your own solution):

. . . .

. . . .

. . . .

DISCUSSION

Having this man released when he has physically recovered (C) is practically signing his death warrant. It is almost certain that he will return to the intravenous use of amphetamines and will die of some complication of this pattern of drug abuse. Even if one were to take the most cold-blooded and pragmatic view of this situation—that is, if this man wants to kill himself in this way, society has no right to stop him—this would still not be a proper choice. This is because there is a significant danger to society that this man may not "go alone." He may, in a state of drug-induced paranoia and instability, kill or injure someone else. This man needs to be protected from himself, and society needs to be protected from him.

Having him released on the condition he seek psychotherapy and not use amphetamines (B) is also a poor choice. Treating this man on an ambulatory basis is as appropriate as doing open-heart surgery in a cafeteria. He is a very sick man. He is a danger to himself and to society. He should be committed to an institution (whether he agrees or not) for long-term psychotherapy (A). It must be emphasized at this point that even the most vigorous and well-designed therapeutic program may not be able to rehabilitate this man. His condition is very close to the common-sense definition, but not necessarily the legal one, of criminal insanity. You may or may not be able to help him recover, but you have to protect him and society from the effects of his illness.

CASE 4-5

A twenty-five year-old woman comes to your office for a checkup after her husband came home one day and found her unconscious on the kitchen floor. She says that nothing is wrong with her except her nerves; lately she has been feeling "frazzled" and ready to go to pieces. She does not look well and appears emaciated, exhausted, and older than her stated age. She has obviously been neglecting herself.

When you ask her to tell you more about herself, she relates that she got married right after she graduated from high school. Her husband is seven years older than she is and is a high school teacher. She has two children, aged seven and five.

She hesitantly begins to tell you that when the children were smaller, being alone with them all day would really get on her nerves, and she was given some tranquilizers by another doctor. This helped her, but she was unable to get out of bed in the morning and felt tired all day. She began to take amphetamines to overcome her fatigue, but they made her nervous so she had to take more tranquilizers during the day and sleeping pills to fall asleep at night. She says that she doesn't know what to do. She doesn't want to take all of these pills, but she is afraid of what will happen if she stops.

In this situation what would you do?

(A) Suggest immediate hospitalization.

(B) Prescribe a major tranquilizer.

(C) Refer her for psychological evaluation and therapy.

(D) Suggest the following (write your own solution):

112

. . . .

. . . .

. . . .

. . . .

. . . .

DISCUSSION

Prescribing a major tranquilizer (B) is obviously inappropriate. The last thing this woman needs at this point is another self-administered medication.

Referral for psychological evaluation and therapy (C) would be desirable, but it is too late for such a course alone to be sufficient. Often one can do very little to resolve a drug-dependent person's underlying problems until one has detoxified him. This is certainly the case here.

This woman is very ill. She has a multiple drug dependence, often called "ups and downs." The detoxification of such a person may be an extremely complicated problem in medical and psychiatric management. It should only be undertaken in a carefully controlled hospital environment (A). The withdrawal syndrome from the depressant drugs can be life-threatening, and the depression associated with withdrawal from amphetamines can lead to suicide attempts. Once these crises have been passed, psychological rehabilitation and family counseling are clearly indicated. But this woman's physical well-being, in what can literally be a life-or-death situation, must be considered first. Only afterwards can you attempt to deal with her underlying problems, e.g., with psychotherapy. In certain situations, you must treat the symptoms of a disease before you can begin a long-term rehabilitative program. This is one of those situations.

On the other hand, this patient might reject hospital detoxification. In that event the physician has only the far less satisfactory alternative of seeing her on an outpatient basis with the aim or the hope of gradually reducing her dependence. The same therapeutic sequence must still apply. The patient must first be helped to get into a drug-free situation before effective rehabilitation can begin. This first stage of help, which cannot be called "psychotherapy," might require months or even years. This sequence is analogous to the one required for many alcoholics.

NOTES

1. J. H. Jaffe, "Drug Addiction and Drug Abuse," in *The Pharmacological Basis of Therapeutics,* 4th edition, ed. L. S. Goodman and S. Gilman (New York: Macmillan Company, 1970), pp. 293–96.

2. "Dependence on Amphetamines and Other Stimulant Drugs," *Journal of the American Medical Association* 197, no. 12 (19 September 1966): 1024.

3. Jaffe, "Drug Addiction and Drug Abuse," pp. 293–96.

4. *Ibid.*

5. *Ibid.*

6. B. P. Citron *et al.,* "Necrotizing Angiitis Associated with Drug Abuse," *New England Journal of Medicine* 283, no. 19 (5 Illicit Drug Market," *Science* 167 (27 February 1970): 1276.

Chapter 5
HALLUCINOGENS

The hallucinogens include a great number of drugs that have similar effects. The most common and most widely used hallucinogen is LSD (lysergic acid diethylamide). It is in many ways the typical hallucinogen, and the one about which the most is known; and it can be used as a model for discussing the whole group. Other common hallucinogens include psilocybin (a dimethyl derivative of 4-hydroxytryptamine, occurring naturally in a Mexican mushroom); DMT (dimethyltryptamine); DET (diethyltryptamine); DOM or STP (2,5-dimethoxy-4-methylamphetamine); MDA (3,4-methylene dioxyamphetamine); and mescaline (3,4,5-trimethoxyphenylethylamine, which occurs naturally in peyote cactus). LSD, psilocybin, DMT, and DET are members of a chemical group known as the indole amines and are structurally related to serotonin (5-hydroxytryptamine), a substance found in certain areas of the brain. Mescaline, MDA, and STP are substituted amphetamines and are structurally related to norepinephrine, which is also found in the brain and in certain nerves.

Hallucinogens are sometimes called psychedelic (mind-manifesting), psychotomimetic (psychosis-mimicking), or psychotogenic (psychosis-producing) drugs because in most users they seem to produce an effect that is mind-altering and that may be perceived as similar to a psychosis. Furthermore, their chemical similarity to endogenous brain chemicals has led some to propose a connection between schizophrenia and a hypothetical "abnormal metabolite" in the brain, which is a hallucinogen-like substance responsible for behavioral disturbances. Clinical and experimental support for this hypothesis has been unconvincing.

Mescaline was the first hallucinogen to be used in North America. Some groups of Southwest American Indians considered mescaline-containing peyote to be the product of the sacred cactus. Peyote is used now as a sacrament in the Native American Church, which was founded by and for American Indians in 1918.[1] LSD was first synthesized in 1938, but it was not until 1943 that its hallucinogenic effects were accidentally discovered. It is the most potent hallucinogen (by dose) known. The usual dose is 100–400 *micro*grams, but even 20–25 micrograms will create hallucinogenic effects in some individuals. Tolerance to the effects of LSD does develop, but its degree and persistence are not well delineated at the present time. There is also cross-tolerance between LSD, mescaline, psilocybin, and other hallucinogens.

All of the hallucinogens are usually taken orally. They all have similar physical and psychological effects. Using LSD as an example, the physical effects of the hallucinogens are basically sympathomimetic. They include tremors, tachycardia, mydriasis (dilation of the pupil), and prevention of sleep. The psychological effects of LSD include changes in perception and mood. They can lead to euphoria or dysphoria, depending entirely upon:

1. the personality of the user;
2. the predrug emotional state of the user;
3. the dose;
4. the immediate surroundings;
5. succeeding events;
6. unknown factors, possibly including genetic constitution.

It is impossible to predict the outcome of an experience with LSD, a "trip," although only a small minority of trips, probably 10 percent or less, have negative or harmful outcomes. Some clinical researchers feel that in optimum circumstances the incidence of bad trips could be reduced to less than 1 percent.

The LSD drug state is characterized by vivid awareness, altered perception, and intense clarity, in the presence of decreased control. Boundaries become fluid, the familiar becomes novel, and the commonplace becomes unique. Any object, event, or thought that comes to one's attention takes on a meaning and importance of its own. Qualities become disembodied; redness becomes more important than that which is red. Simple thoughts and statements require a cosmic profundity in a religious, aesthetic, sensual, philosophic, or mixed frame of reference. Laughing, crying, or both together are very common, and may reflect no objective or subjective affect or mood. The ego is less in control of mood, perception, or action. Defenses are weakened, and one is more vulnerable to a wide range of external or internal events. This situation can overwhelm the individual with a resultant total loss of control. This has been called the "dying of the ego." For some this can result in the worst possible bad trip, but for others it becomes a transcendental, mystical experience. The experiences of the drug state are fully remembered afterwards. Whether an LSD experience is perceived as a good one or a bad one depends on all of the six factors mentioned above. Some persons literally never recover from an LSD experience. It may be that these people were on the verge of a breakdown before the drug and that the drug merely brought to light a basic defect. Nevertheless, there are a few individuals (and it is only a few) in whom LSD precipitates a psychotic break. It must be remembered that a bad experience does not necessarily lead to a bad outcome; but the unpredictability of these drugs and the fact that self-examination or confrontation with personal problems as a motive for the drug-taking commonly leads to bad trips clearly represent dangers inherent in indiscriminate or even discriminate use of them.

Some of the ill effects of LSD have already been mentioned. Others include a panicked psychotic state, which usually clears as the drug effect disappears, and recurrences ("flashbacks"). A recurrence is a return of the drug effect without taking the drug again. This can come days, weeks, or even months after even a single dose of LSD. For some persons, these recurrences are a source of anxiety and of fear of the loss of sanity. No one knows why they happen, but recurrences often seem to be triggered by intoxication with another drug, such as alcohol or marihuana. Recurrences do not forecast insanity and are only dangerous (as is the LSD trip itself) if the response to a recurrence is panic or breakdown. Recurrences usually disappear spontaneously; if they do not disappear, an underlying psychosis may be responsible. However, little is known either about the actual cause of recurrences or the long-term psychiatric complications of LSD intoxication.

There have been no human deaths attributed to an overdose of LSD, but suicides and fatal accidents have occurred among persons under the influence of the drug. In animals toxic overdose produces death following a series of convulsive seizures.

The concepts of craving, compulsive abuse, and withdrawal symptoms do not apply to the hallucinogens as they do to the drugs that depress the central nervous system. But when an individual devotes much time to self-intoxication with hallucinogens, adverse behavioral effects may be just as serious as those associated with compulsive abuse or addiction.

QUESTIONS

1. Hallucinogens are not addicting drugs.

    True or false? . . . . . .

2. The hallucinogens have no legitimate use.

    True or false? . . . . . .

3. It is possible to have a bad experience with LSD, following one or several good experiences with the drug.

    True or false? . . . . . .

4. A bad experience ("bad trip") with LSD leads to insanity.

    True or false? . . . . . .

5. One of the dangers of the illicit use of hallucinogens is the misrepresentation of both the dosage and the actual type of hallucinogen being sold.

    True or false? . . . . . .

6. LSD causes chromosome damage in man.

    True or false? . . . . . .

7. The state produced by the hallucinogens is identical to a naturally occurring psychosis.

    True or false? . . . . . .

ANSWERS

1. Hallucinogens are not addicting drugs.

Answer: *True*. While theoretically possible for any euphorigenic psychoactive drug, addiction to hallucinogens is uncommon if not rare. The dangers of hallucinogen use are not the dangers of drug addiction or drug dependence, but rather the possibility of harmful consequences from even a single experience with these agents—or the possibility of adverse effects of repeated experiences on brain function. The possible adverse effects on brain function of repeated use of hallucinogens is only beginning to be investigated.

2. The hallucinogens have no legitimate use.

Answer: *False*. Hallucinogens are very important research tools in the study of brain chemistry and of abnormal brain states such as psychosis. Furthermore, some physicians have been using LSD experimentally as an adjunct in certain types of psychotherapy. Such use of LSD is very controversial, and none of these agents is available by prescription in the United States. They must be obtained by government approval and for research purposes only.

3. It is possible to have a bad experience with LSD, following one or several good experiences with the drug.

Answer: *True*. One good trip does not predict another. Because the quality of the LSD experience depends so much on the pre-drug emotional state of the user, his immediate surroundings, and succeeding events, it is impossible to predict the outcome of an experience with LSD.

122

4. A bad experience ("bad trip") with LSD leads to insanity.

Answer: *False*. Most bad trips do not lead to "insanity," i.e., they do not result in chronic psychotic illness. It is possible that those few who suffer that fate would have become psychotic later following some other adverse experience. The majority of bad trips certainly leave a profound impact on the personality—whether for good or ill is to some extent controversial, and adequate psychiatric evaluation of such cases has not yet been accomplished.

5. One of the dangers of the illicit use of hallucinogens is the misrepresentation of both the dosage and the actual type of hallucinogen being sold.

Answer: *True*. In a study done in New York City,[2] thirty-six samples of different street drugs were analyzed as to their true contents. Only fourteen of the thirty-six were actually what they were alleged to be, that is, LSD, but the doses varied from 50 micrograms to 283 micrograms. One other sample, alleged to be LSD, was not. All of the samples sold as LSD were supposed to contain 250 micrograms of the drug. The one sample alleged to be THC was actually MDA. Of the fourteen samples alleged to be mescaline, seven were LSD, four were STP, one was aspirin, and two were unidentified. Of the five samples that were alleged to be psilocybin, four were LSD and one was unidentified.

6. LSD causes chromosome damage in man.

Answer: *False*. Although some early reports indicated that LSD caused chromosome damage in laboratory cultures of human cells, later studies have shown that chromosome damage occurs neither in laboratory cultures of human cells nor in human beings given doses of LSD.[3] Furthermore, other studies have shown that women who have taken LSD have no higher percentage of abortions, stillbirths, or malformed babies than do women who have not taken LSD.[4] Although all of the evidence is not yet available, the preponderance of the evidence indicates that LSD does not cause genetic damage in humans.[5]

7. The state produced by the hallucinogens is identical to a naturally occurring psychosis.

Answer: *False*. Although visual and tactile hallucinations may occur in both a natural psychosis and a hallucinogenically induced state of altered consciousness, the drug-induced progression and pattern of visual distortion rarely, if ever, occurs in a natural psychosis. Furthermore, auditory manifestations, which are very common in a natural psychosis, rarely occur in the drug-induced state.

CASE 5-1

A twenty-two year-old woman comes to see you. She tells you that she has always been somewhat nervous, but that recently things have become much worse. Four months ago her husband, who has taken LSD many times without any problems, persuaded her to try some. She didn't have a particularly bad experience, but since then she has had several "flashbacks" which have really frightened her.

When you ask her to tell you more about these flashbacks, she reports that she can tell when one is coming on by the funny feeling she gets in her body. She had the same feeling, she says, while under the influence of LSD. She reports that she gets a fluttery feeling in her heart and that things start looking distorted, as they did on her "trip." She says she's very worried that she's going crazy or that something is wrong with her heart and she will die.

The last episode of this nature occurred two weeks ago, after she had been drinking at a party. Since then, she has been very nervous and constantly worries about when the next episode will come and what such episodes mean. She denies any drug use other than alcohol since she had the LSD, and she mentions that several of the flashbacks have occurred after drinking, but that some have come out of nowhere.

A physical examination reveals a thin, nervous female with no evidence of organic disease, including heart disease. The "fluttering" she feels in her heart during a flashback is very likely due to a tachycardia (increase in heart rate) and is secondary to her anxiety about the flashback rather than to any disease process.

She asks you to give her something for nerves.
If you were the doctor, what would you do?

(A) Prescribe a minor tranquilizer.
(B) Prescribe a major tranquilizer.
(C) Refer her for psychological evaluation and therapy.
(D) Reassure her that "flashbacks" are not uncommon,
     that they are not a sign of insanity or impending in-
     sanity, and that they often are precipitated by the
     use of other drugs.
(E) Suggest that she be hospitalized for rehabilitation.
(F) Suggest the following (write your own solution):

. . . .

. . . .

. . . .

. . . .

. . . .

DISCUSSION

Giving this woman any kind of tranquilizer (A or B) at this point would be a mistake. She needs reassurance, more than medication. Further thoughts on this subject may be found in the discussion of Case 3-3.

The proper course of action at this time is to reassure her that "flashbacks" from LSD are not uncommon, that they are not a sign of insanity or impending insanity, and that they are often precipitated by the use of other drugs, such as alcohol (D). This simple reassurance may not by itself eliminate her flashback episodes, but it may reduce her anxieties about them. If this woman abstains from other drugs, these episodes will very likely disappear. A followup visit in one or two months should be arranged, but she should be seen sooner if the episodes do not begin to subside.

If the episodes persist, the proper course would be either psychological evaluation and treatment on an ambulatory basis (C) or as an inpatient in a hospital (E), depending on the severity of her complaints. However, these steps should not be taken before further reassurance is attempted. The physician at this point must have sufficient training and experience to know how far he should go in investigating this woman's psychological problems. There should be sufficient understanding to provide identification of the specific fears that are associated with the flashback experience. Escalation of psychological treatment approaches must be appropriate and measured. An aggressive approach may be counterproductive if the patient is led to panic by the idea that the drug has seriously damaged her mind.

CASE 5-2

You are working in the emergency room of a hospital when a seventeen year-old male is brought in by a group of youths. He is in acute distress and is screaming, shouting, and thrashing wildly about. The young men tell you that he took some LSD about two hours ago and "is on a bummer." They also tell you that he had taken LSD twice before and had not "freaked out," and they don't know what to do.

You have him placed in a room and have one of his friends wait with him. By this time he has calmed down some, but as you enter the room you find him huddled in the corner, quietly sobbing and whimpering.

If you were the doctor, what would you do?

(A) Try to take a history from him and do a physical examination to rule out a non-drug-related organic basis for his condition.

(B) Administer an injection of chlorpromazine (Thorazine).

(C) Arrange to have him placed in restraints or a straight-jacket to prevent him from injuring himself.

(D) Reassure him quietly and gently that he will be all right as soon as the effects of the drug wear off.

(E) Suggest the following (write your own solution):

. . . .

. . . .

. . . .

. . . .

128

DISCUSSION

Trying to take a history and doing a physical examination to rule out a non-drug-related organic basis for his condition (A) is probably not a good idea. This young man's condition may preclude any cooperation on his part. There is no reason to believe that he would or could be a more reliable historian than his friends. Furthermore, any physical manipulation, especially by a stranger in a white coat, could be extremely frightening and threatening to someone in his state. Such a course could precipitate a very severe panic reaction and yet not be helpful in the treatment of the young man's problems.

Placing him in restraints or in a straight-jacket to prevent him from injuring himself (C) should be used only as a last resort. This is also a threatening and frightening procedure, even to someone who is not psychologically disturbed. Besides, when you enter the room he has already calmed down. He is probably in no danger of injuring himself, or anyone else, unless by inappropriate actions you provoke a panic reaction. However, panic reactions depend upon how you are perceived by the patient, and this is sometimes beyond your power to control.

Administering an injection of chlorpromazine (B) has two drawbacks. Like the other courses of action we have discussed, an injection may provoke a panic reaction. Furthermore, although chlorpromazine is fairly effective in ameliorating the effects of a "bad trip" due to LSD, it aggravates a bad reaction to STP. With the present uncertainty about the true composition of hallucinogens being sold on the street, regardless of what they are said to be, it is unwise to take the risk of aggravating an already bad situation by inappropriate medication. This is especially true since medication is usually not necessary to treat "bad trips." The majority of "bummers" are panic reactions and respond very well to quiet and gentle reassurance that the person will be all right as soon as the effects of the drug wear off (D). Such people should be told that what they are experiencing is a drug effect and that it is not due to any change in reality or to their losing their sanity.

In order to preserve his sometimes tenuous contact with reality, someone may have to spend many hours in reassuring this young man. Often the mere presence of another person who is not under the influence of LSD can prevent a "bad trip." However, there are cases in which such conservative therapy is ineffective and where these reactions may persist for days, weeks, or longer. Such reactions are treated by methods similar to those used for other psychotic reactions. They may be due to an underlying psychosis or disturbance, a genetic propensity towards such reactions, or some other as yet undiscovered causes.

CASE 5-3

An eighteen year-old girl is brought to see you by her parents. They tell you that she has been acting strangely for the past three days, when, according to her friends, she took LSD for the first time. Her father says that his daughter was always high-strung, but she has never been like this. He says that these past few days she has been withdrawn, uncommunicative, and has been "seeing things." At first, they hoped that it would clear up by itself, but they haven't been able to get through to her at all.

All this time the girl has been looking at the wall behind you and has been alternately staring blankly and grimacing animatedly. You ask her parents to wait outside for awhile, and you try to communicate with the girl. At first she ignores everything you say, not even looking at you, but then she suddenly becomes somewhat agitated and begins a monologue. She asks over and over again, why won't they leave her alone, why won't they go away. When you try to ask her who "they" are, she just says, "If you were my friend you would make them go away."

In this situation what would you do?

(A) Refer her for psychiatric evaluation and therapy.
(B) Refer the parents to a family counselor.
(C) Reassure the parents that this is just an adolescent phase she is passing through.
(D) Suggest the following (write your own solution):

. . . .

. . . .

. . . .

. . . .

. . . .

DISCUSSION

This is obviously not the manifestation of an "adolescent phase" (C) that this girl is passing through. She should be psychiatrically evaluated immediately and treated according to the evaluation (A). Such an evaluation would probably indicate that hospitalization is necessary for this girl's rehabilitation. Family counseling (B) would probably help the parents cope with this situation, but this alternative alone would do little for the girl's problems. Such family counseling should be prescribed on the basis of the parents' problems, rather than for the girl's problems; and the recommendation should be made only after other arrangements for the girl's treatment have been settled.

CASE 5-4

A twenty-two year-old woman comes to see you because she thinks she is pregnant. The laboratory tests confirm that she is, and she asks you to be her obstetrician. You take a preliminary history and do a physical, both of which are unremarkable. When you ask her if she has any questions, she says "Yes," and begins to tell you her concerns.

Both she and her husband have taken LSD many times. They have used LSD to "explore inner space" and have had some "interesting and illuminating experiences." Both she and her husband are college graduates. He is a graduate student, and she is working as a research assistant in the university. Neither have had any "bum trips" or bad after-effects from the drug, but she is worried about the possibility of the LSD having affected either her or her husband's chromosomes, so they might produce a deformed child. She says that she and her husband want very much to have children, but that she really doesn't like to think about it, because what is done can't be changed, but she can't help but wonder if her baby will be normal.

If you were the doctor, what would you do?

(A) Suggest that she get an abortion.

(B) Reassure her that her baby will have the same chance of being normal as anyone else's.

(C) Refer her for psychological evaluation and therapy.

(D) Suggest hospitalization for rehabilitation.

(E) Suggest the following (write your own solution):

. . . .

. . . .

. . . .

. . . .

. . . .

DISCUSSION

Psychological evaluation and therapy (C) or hospitalization for rehabilitation (D) are both inappropriate here. This woman has a rational concern about the possible consequences of her previous actions. At this time, she does not manifest any inappropriate reactions to her situation. However, if, in the future, this situation should change, either (C) or (D) should be considered.

Her anxiety stems from a fear that her child will in some way be abnormal. This is a common fear in most pregnant women. The proper course of action in this case would be to tell her that her baby will have the same chance of being normal as anyone else's (B). The latest evidence concerning the possibilities of genetic damage to human beings as a result of LSD use suggests that LSD neither significantly affects chromosomes in human cell cultures nor alters the probability or incidence of birth defects. This evidence should be used to reassure this woman.

However, it should be mentioned that the first three months of pregnancy are a critical period in the development of the unborn child. Because we know so little about the effects of drugs on developing fetuses, the common medical policy is to avoid all but absolutely essential medications during this period. Although LSD has not been conclusively shown to cause congenital malformations, it would be sensible to avoid the use of this drug, as well as almost all others, during pregnancy.

Uncertainty about the identity of illegal drugs is the most realistic potential danger for the fetus. Nevertheless, the actuality of this danger is not substantial enough to merit recommendation of an abortion (A). If this issue comes up, however, and if this woman panics, it may be necessary to consider a therapeutic abortion, but only if it can be regarded as a last resort to prevent serious mental breakdown.

NOTES

1. M. E. Jarvik, "Drugs Used in the Treatment of Psychiatric Disorders," in *The Pharmacological Basis of Therapeutics,* 4th edition, ed. L. S. Goodman and A. Gilman (New York: Macmillan Company, 1970), p. 195.

2. F. E. Cheek, S. Newell, and M. Joffe, "Deceptions in the Illicit Drug Market," *Science* 167 (27 February 1970): 1276.

3. See M. J. Corey *et al.,* "Chromosome Studies on Patients (In Vivo) and Cells (In Vitro) Treated with Lysergic Acid Diethylamide," *New England Journal of Medicine* 282, no. 17 (23 April 1970): 939–43.

4. See W. H. McGlothin, R. S. Sparkes, and D. O. Arnold, "Effect of LSD on Human Pregnancy," *Journal of the American Medical Association* 212, no. 9 (1 June 1970): 1483–87.

5. For a comprehensive review, see N. I. Dishotsky *et al.,* "LSD and Genetic Damage," *Science* 172 (30 April 1971): 431–40.

Chapter 6

MARIHUANA

Marihuana is the dried leaves and flowering tops of the hemp plant (genus cannabis). Contrary to common belief, an important recent study shows that the male and female parts of the plant are equally potent for any given strain.[1] The active ingredient of marihuana is presently thought to be Δ^1–tetrahydrocannabinol (THC). The potency of the preparation is directly correlated with the THC content. The THC concentration in marihuana or hashish (the resin of the plant) may vary over a 100-fold range. Recent evidence suggests that growing conditions and climate do not affect the variation in the THC concentration. Variation in the THC concentration depends mainly on the genetics of the strain.[2] The average orally effective dose of THC is 3.5–15 mg; but when smoked, the average effective dose is 1.5–3.5 mg, or even less. Inactivation and/or incomplete absorption of the THC in the gastrointestinal tract contribute to the relative ineffectiveness of oral dosing. Smoking marihuana or hashish is the most common form of THC use. Not only is the effect achieved more rapidly when smoked, but smoking converts THC acids to the pharmacologically active THC. The complexity of the synthesis of THC has acted as a bar to its availability on the illegal market.

The physical effects of THC smoked as marihuana include tachycardia (rapid heart rate) and conjunctivitis (redness of the eyes). There is no change in respiratory rate, pupil size, or blood sugar level. In contrast to alcohol, hypnotics, and tranquilizers, marihuana affects motor function only in high doses. The effect of low doses is primarily in the realm of feeling and thought. Both experienced and inexperienced users demonstrate impaired performance on certain psychological tests that were specifically designed for this drug. It has not yet been determined to what extent marihuana intoxication impairs driving performance.

The psychological effects of marihuana are dependent on the following:

1. the user's experience or inexperience with the drug;
2. the personality of the user;
3. the route of administration;
4. the dose;
5. the circumstances surrounding the drug use.

Except for the first item, this list is nearly identical to the list previously given for the hallucinogens. The psychological effects of marihuana in the small doses normally used resemble the effects of hallucinogens, but are much more subtle. A major difference is that to a large extent the psychological effects of marihuana can be overcome or reversed voluntarily. (This applies only to small doses, and it would be true of a small dose of any drug.) The user is often able to remain objective and is more in control of the drug effect than he is after use of the hallucinogens.

The inexperienced user of marihuana will often notice some alterations in perception and may describe the effects as a weird dizziness. The experienced user may well have the same feelings, but he will tend to define these feelings as pleasurable. He will also notice an increased appetite and thirst, and he will describe a heightened awareness and enhanced sensation: music seems to sound better, food tastes better, objects look more interesting, and so on. In the experienced user, marihuana seems to have the effect of an emotional-sensory amplifier. The user will preoccupy himself with only one aspect of a picture, thought, sound, or taste, to the total exclusion of other perceptions. Furthermore, if the user is happy, he may feel happier under the influence of the drug; but if a depressed person smokes marihuana, he is likely to become more depressed. These effects are mild, and it is likely that they are due to a measure of autosuggestion that may be facilitated by the drug's effect on the brain.

In both inexperienced and experienced users, marihuana can also cause what has been called temporal disintegration. This may be related to an interference with the short-term memory function of the brain.[3] Temporal disintegration is associated with the user's common inability to estimate the passage of time accurately and with his difficulty in carrying on a detailed conversation while under the influence of marihuana.

High doses of THC produce hallucinogenic effects. However, THC does not produce the sympathomimetic effects characteristic of the hallucinogens and exhibits no cross-tolerance with LSD. Furthermore, high doses of THC, especially when smoked, have a marked sedative effect. Unlike the hallucinogens, which do not permit sleep, the person intoxicated with marihuana can readily doze off.[4] The chain smoking of high-potency marihuana, although it is not common in the U.S., results in a prolonged coma.[5]

It would, therefore, seem appropriate to put the THC drugs in a class of their own, separate from the hallucinogens.

The effects of smoking marihuana reach their maximum intensity within a half hour, diminish within one hour, and have usually disappeared three hours after smoking. Oral ingestion of marihuana or hashish often produces somewhat different subjective effects than those produced by smoking these drugs. The onset of these effects is one hour or more after ingestion, and the duration of the effects is five to six hours.

The evidence for tolerance to THC is ambiguous, but observations in North Africa, where higher doses are used, suggest that tolerance occurs in man. Laboratory studies clearly indicate that tolerance develops in many animal species.[6] Some users report the occurrence of what they call reverse tolerance. They maintain the more experience a person has had with marihuana, the less one requires to become intoxicated. A great deal of ongoing research is directed toward elucidating the pharmacology of THC. Such questions as the distribution, metabolism, and excretion of THC in man will probably be greatly clarified in the next few years. Some recent research has demonstrated a two-phase biological half-life of THC in humans. During the rapid phase, which lasts about thirty minutes, the drug is distributed throughout the body. This is followed by the second, or slow, phase, during which the drug disappears with a half-life of up to fifty-six hours.[7] This slow, secondary, biological half-life of THC in humans may be indicative of a cumulative "storage" of THC in the body and may be related to the subjective accounts of reverse tolerance that have been reported.

Physical dependence (producing withdrawal symptoms), or craving, has been observed following abrupt cessation of marihuana use. But the intensity of the symptoms is much less than those associated with alcohol, hypnotics, and tranquilizers.[8] Most medical authorities agree that marihuana does not directly cause criminal behavior, juvenile delinquency, sexual excitement, or the use of other drugs.[9] Since 1937, marihuana and other cannabis derivatives have been listed as narcotics, along with heroin and morphine, in the federal narcotics laws. The possession, use, and sale of marihuana are felonies, with very severe penalties. However, in certain jurisdictions, new legislation has been adopted that reduces some of these offenses to misdemeanors. Pharmacologically, marihuana is not a narcotic, but neither is it an innocuous drug. In the near future, the laws may be changed to conform more accurately to the scientific classification of marihuana. An estimated twelve and possibly twenty million people in this country have smoked marihuana at least once, although the number of regular users is estimated to be much smaller.[10]

Adverse reactions to the acute use of marihuana do occur, although infrequently. In persons with a history of psychosis, marihuana can trigger a psychotic episode. Such episodes can also be triggered in these people by other drugs, such as alcohol, amphetamines, and LSD. The therapy for these episodes is the same as the therapy for other psychoses. In persons with no history of mental illness, but who have taken a hallucinogen, marihuana can precipitate a recurrence of the hallucinogen's effects.

In persons who have no history of mental illness and who have never taken a hallucinogen, three adverse reactions to marihuana have been observed. All three reactions are self-limited; should be treated with appropriate reassurance, not drugs; and always end spontaneously. The first, a depressive reaction, most often occurs in obsessive-compulsive persons. The second, a panic reaction, frequently occurs in novice users and older persons, usually those who have ambivalent feelings about marihuana. This reaction is not a psychosis, and it responds especially well to reassurance. Such panic reactions account for about 75 percent of all adverse reactions to marihuana. The third, a temporary toxic psychosis, never occurs following smoking, because the user falls asleep before the required dose can be smoked. The psychosis follows oral ingestion of high doses of marihuana or hashish. The psychosis is not dangerous, and it clears spontaneously, without any need for medication.[11]

A recent study has reported several cases of young people

who developed psychotic episodes or adverse changes of behavior (loss of motivation, sexual promiscuity, homosexuality) after regular use of marihuana.[12] The basic observations indicated that the patients were well before using marihuana but suffered various kinds of behavioral deteriorations while on the drug, and that of those who stopped using it most returned to the pre-drug state. Typical findings included apathy, withdrawal, confusion, memory impairment, depression, and paranoia. Criticisms of this study center on (1) lack of pharmacological control, since only the patient's history was used to rule out use of drugs other than marihuana; and (2) statistical bias, since the authors are psychiatrists, whose subjects were automatically selected on the basis of their having psychiatric symptoms. On the other hand, lack of pharmacological control is the "rule" on the street. The study suggests that some chemical (unspecified) is causing adverse effects in the group that they studied. It is possible that these effects were actually produced by THC, since many of the reported effects are similar to effects observed following administration of a single dose of chemically defined THC. This study has value because it describes what may happen to some moderate or heavy users of marihuana, but it cannot indicate *how often* such adverse effects occur. More systematic observations of marihuana-using groups may answer some of these questions.

An even more alarming British study has suggested that heavy use of cannabis can lead to cerebral atrophy (shrinkage of the brain).[13] This irreversible condition was found in 10 men, average age 22, who were said to have been addicted, heavy users for 3 to 11 years. Cerebral atrophy was revealed by pneumoencephalography, a special skull x-ray procedure that reveals some of the outlines of the brain. All of the patients had serious psychiatric disturbances of a type associated with cerebral atrophy. These included restlessness, irritability, anxiety, confusion, poor memory, and a tendency to be withdrawn and suspicious. Although the cerebral atrophy in these 10 cases is real, it has not been proven that the heavy use of cannabis was the cause. All of these patients had used lesser amounts of LSD or amphetamines. There is also a possibility that cerebral atrophy of whatever cause (although it is rare in young people) may predispose toward the use of cannabis. The chief value of this study is to alert all medical researchers to the need for more systematic neurological studies of all users of psychoactive drugs.

QUESTIONS

1. Marihuana is a narcotic.

   True or false? . . . . . .

2. Marihuana is a hallucinogen.

   True or false? . . . . . .

3. It is impossible to become addicted to marihuana.

   True or false? . . . . . .

4. Marihuana use usually leads to heroin addiction.

True or false? . . . . . .

5. Marihuana increases the sexual drive.

True or false? . . . . . .

6. Marihuana is a harmless drug.

True or false? . . . . . .

ANSWERS

1. Marihuana is a narcotic.

Answer: *False*. Although marihuana and its derivatives are listed under the federal narcotics laws, together with the narcotic analgesics, marihuana is not a narcotic. It really belongs in a class by itself.

2. Marihuana is a hallucinogen.

Answer: *False*. Marihuana and its derivatives share many similarities with the hallucinogens, but there are some major differences between the two groups of drugs. All hallucinogens contain at least one nitrogen atom, but the THC molecule has none. The hallucinogens and marihuana both cause altered perception, but the short-term effects of usual doses of marihuana are much milder than are those of the hallucinogens and are not associated with the marked loss of ego control so common with the hallucinogens. Another difference is that the hallucinogens are like the stimulant drugs in that they do not permit sleep during the drug state and in high doses produce motor excitement and convulsive seizures. Marihuana, however, produces only tachycardia (increased heart rate), has a marked sedative effect, and in high doses produces stupor and coma in the person intoxicated with the drug. These differences notwithstanding, some authorities still classify marihuana and THC as hallucinogens. The classification of psychoactive drugs is useful but somewhat arbitrary. Pharmacologically it is more important to understand the many actions of each individual drug than to be able to classify it.

3. It is impossible to become addicted to marihuana.

147

Answer: *False*. Addiction is a behavior pattern of compulsive drug use, characterized by an overwhelming preoccupation with the use of the drug and securing its supply and by a high tendency to relapse after withdrawal. There are marihuana users whose behavior fits this definition. Their number in the U.S. is unknown. Withdrawal symptoms and craving, if they occur, are of lesser intensity than those associated with narcotics, barbiturates, or alcohol. They are, rather, to be compared in intensity with the withdrawal symptoms and craving associated with tobacco habituation (see Chapter 7).

4. Marihuana use usually leads to heroin addiction.

Answer: *False*. Although many heroin addicts have a history of marihuana use, and although marihuana was thought for a time to lead inevitably to heroin addiction, no cause-and-effect relationship between the use of the two drugs has been proven. However, the danger in the illicit use of marihuana is that acquisition of the drug through *illegal* sources of supply may put a potential abuser of drugs in contact with suppliers of other drugs that are much more dangerous than marihuana. A strong relationship between frequent marihuana use and the use of other drugs has been demonstrated.[14] However, it is not possible to say whether marihuana use is responsible for the use of the other drugs, whether use of other drugs is responsible for marihuana use, or whether neither possibility is true.

5. Marihuana increases the sexual drive.

Answer: *False*. Marihuana probably has no direct, short-term effect on the sexual drive. It is, however, sometimes claimed that marihuana can enhance pleasurable sensations, including those associated with sexual activity. However, there is no way of evaluating the meaning of such a claim. Sexual behavior involves simultaneous increase in excitement and narrowing and focusing of attention on sensations in the sexual organs. There seems no reason to believe that this sequence or its climax can be made more pleasurable by any drug. While occasionally drugs may relieve inhibitions of sexual behavior, adverse effects such as depression, hilarity, and panic are also included in the range of possible responses. The sensations enhanced by marihuana are often not the sexual ones, but the drug-induced, pleasurable intensifications of an ordinary sense may be tantamount to a "sexualization" of that sense. In contrast to the occasional use of marihuana, heavy use of marihuana, or any other dependence-producing psychoactive drug, tends to diminish interest in ordinary sexual activity.

6. Marihuana is a harmless drug.

Answer: *False*. There is actual and potential hazard in the use of any psychoactive drug. Indeed, this is true of any drug. For marihuana, it remains unknown what level of use is associated with significant hazard as well as the specific nature of the hazards. It is known that some people have adverse effects from the acute use of marihuana, and others appear to develop a pattern of psychological dependence on the drug. Also, the use of marihuana by young people as a means of postponing or avoiding the internal conflicts characteristic of adolescence may significantly impair or even arrest the development of a mature personality.

CASE 6-1

A forty-seven year-old man is brought to the emergency room of a hospital in a state of extreme agitation. He says he thinks he's having a heart attack. He is conscious and alert, but he appears very frightened and anxious.

He and his twenty year-old son, who is a college student, had several discussions about marihuana during his son's spring vacation, and he agreed to try it for himself to find out what it was really like. He says he was both apprehensive and curious about it, but his son repeatedly reassured him that marihuana was harmless.

He reports that he smoked several marihuana cigarettes about an hour ago with his son. About thirty minutes later, he says, he felt his heart racing and pounding in his chest, felt dizzy, his mouth felt dry, and he thought he was having a heart attack. This especially frightened him because his father had died of a heart attack at age forty-two.

A physical examination and electrocardiogram show a tachycardia (rapid heart rate), but reveal no signs or symptoms consistent with a heart attack or heart disease.

After reassuring him that he is not having a heart attack, what would you do?

(A) Administer a minor tranquilizer.
(B) Administer a hypnotic sedative.
(C) Tell him that reactions like his are not uncommon, are not dangerous, and that he'll feel better as soon as he stops worrying.
(D) Refer him for psychological evaluation and therapy.

(E) Suggest that he seek family counseling.
(F) Suggest the following (write your own solution):

. . . .

. . . .

. . . .

. . . .

. . . .

DISCUSSION

Administering a minor tranquilizer (A) or a hypnotic sedative (B) is overtreatment of this man's problem. He is having a panic reaction to marihuana. The psychological effects of either of these two kinds of drugs may be interpreted by this man as further evidence of his "mental deterioration" and may even increase his feelings of panic. Also, the acute effects of THC should not be complicated by adding the effects of other drugs.

Panic reactions respond best to appropriate reassurance. It is important to reassure this man that reactions to marihuana, such as he is having, are not uncommon, are not dangerous, and that he'll feel better soon (C). (Coronary disease, however, is common after the age of forty. It is possible that actual heart disorders could co-exist with acute marihuana intoxication. A complete medical evaluation would be appropriate for this man.) The usual duration of the effect of smoked marihuana is from one to three hours. The administration of such agents as sedatives or tranquilizers may prolong the panic reaction. After reassuring this man, you should keep him under observation for an hour or two until the drug effects disappear. At this time, you should evaluate his psychological status. You may, at this time, depending on the situation, decide to refer him for psychological evaluation and therapy (D) or family counseling (E). In most cases, such action may not be necessary. The important point to note is that these actions are to be taken only after the acute problem, the panic reaction, has been dealt with. Only after this has been done can you, on the basis of the success or failure of your initial treatment and the man's subsequent psychological status, proceed with appropriate long-term treatment.

CASE 6-2

A forty-one year-old man and his thirty-eight year-old wife have come to see you about their seventeen year-old son. They are obviously upset and embarrassed to be in this situation. The mother reports that a week ago she found an envelope hidden in her son's underwear drawer. She thought it was marihuana, but neither she nor her husband knew for sure. They decided to confront their son with her discovery and ask him what it was. When they did so, he told them yes, it was marihuana, and that he had been smoking it for about a year. They were very upset about his reply, and they asked him if he didn't know that marihuana is dangerous and leads to heroin and LSD use. He told his parents they didn't know what they were talking about. Since then, they have been avoiding arguments only by avoiding each other, but they did agree to seek outside advice from someone they could all trust. When you ask the parents if they have noticed a change in their son's grades, habits, or behavior over the past year, they reply no, that he has always been a good student, is clean in his personal habits, and gets along well with people. They also say that before this, they always felt fortunate because they had never had any trouble with him.

You ask the parents to wait outside, and you call the son in to see you. He is an alert, intelligent, well-developed young man, who looks clean and healthy. He is polite, but somewhat subdued, and he conveys the impression that he doesn't really trust you.

When you ask him about his situation, he gives you essentially the same story his parents presented. He is angry with his mother for "snooping around," but he seems to think

153

he would have been discovered sooner or later. He says he is most upset about the fact that his parents think there is something wrong with him and are full of misinformation. He asks you to "straighten them out."

When you ask him about his use of marihuana, he replies that he first smoked about a year ago. For about a month, he smoked almost every day; but after that, he got tired of it. It wasn't that he didn't feel the effects of the drug, but after a while it just wasn't interesting any more. Since then he has smoked two or three times a month, usually at parties or with friends. He denies use of any other drugs, including narcotics, amphetamines, alcohol, barbiturates, and hallucinogens. He feels his parents, like most adults, are hypocrites because they drink alcohol but frown on marihuana use. He says he would rather smoke marihuana than smoke cigarettes or drink alcohol because it's less harmful. He asks you to explain to his parents that he's not a "drug freak" and to get them "off his back" about it.

In this situation, what would you do?

Suggest your own solution.

. . . .

. . . .

. . . .

. . . .

DISCUSSION

Your approach to this situation should take into consideration that it is, at this time, primarily a problem in family communication rather than a problem of drug dependence. A good approach would be to speak with the boy and his parents together. You should reassure the parents that you think their son is basically a well-adjusted young man and that this judgment is based on the fact that he seems to be functioning well in his environment and exhibits none of the signs of drug-dependent behavior. You should explain that an important danger inherent in his use of marihuana is the possibility of prosecution resulting in severe legal penalties. This factor cannot be overlooked. In the absence of such complications, *this* pattern of marihuana use is not likely to lead to any acute physical or psychological damage. If continued over a long period of time, however, you can offer no reassurance about the absence of any adverse chronic mental or physical effects. You should also tell them that although you understand his use of marihuana, you nevertheless cannot condone it. You should add that it is, however, his decision to make and that you feel he is mature enough to make the proper decision himself.

You should also point out to the son that his parents bringing him to see you was a significant manifestation of their concern for his welfare and that they mean him no harm. You should add that although problems like this one are fairly common in adolescence, the way to avoid such problems in the future is to maintain open communication between his parents and him. Such communication is attainable only in the presence of mutual respect and a willingness to compromise.

This is everyone's responsibility. Shouting and screaming will not solve this family's communication problem, but rather the kind of reasonable conversation that results when people who respect each other discuss their differences.

Finally, you should mention that if they have any further questions or problems, they should feel free to call on you in the future.

CASE 6-3

A sixteen year-old boy is brought to see you by his parents. In the past six months, a great change has come over him. Until then, he was always "a good student and a nice boy." Since then, he has become slovenly in his appearance, lazy and disobedient, and his grades have dropped sharply. They are very worried about him and are embarrassed about having to seek outside help.

You ask them to wait outside while you talk to their son. When he comes in, you see a well-developed sixteen year-old. He looks somewhat withdrawn and contemptuous of you. His clothes are dirty, his hair is long and unkempt, and he looks as if he has been neglecting his personal hygiene.

When you ask him about his appearance, he replies that it's because the hypocrisy and stupidity of the older generation finally "got to him," and he felt he couldn't take it any more and had to do something to show he was different. He says his parents, their friends, the schools, and adults in general stand for all the wrong things and don't really understand the younger generation.

When you ask him about drug use, he laughs and says, "I'm not that stupid," but does admit to smoking marihuana regularly several times a week for the past six months. He says "getting stoned" helps him understand himself better; what the world needs, he says, is more "potheads" and fewer alcoholics.

In this situation, what would you do?
Suggest your own solution.

. . . .

. . . .

. . . .

. . . .

. . . .

DISCUSSION

This case is not like the previous one. This young man is not coping with his environment as effectively as is the young man in Case 6-2. It is difficult to say how much of this is related to his use of marihuana. On the one hand, his change in behavior may be due in large part to a rebellious phase of his adolescence. On the other hand, it may be a manifestation of a deeper psychological problem, which is being aggravated by a possible marihuana dependence. The first priority in this case is the establishment of a trusting relationship between you and the boy. This means that you will have to see him alone for a while. You should let him know that you will not tell his parents anything unless you both agree about what they should be told. You should, of course, tell the parents that more sessions with the boy and perhaps with them will be necessary.

Once you are firmly along the way toward the desired relationship, you should attempt to discover to what extent this boy's use of marihuana has complicated his problems. Any further action on your part should be determined, in large part, by what you discover. This situation may be the manifestation of a personality disturbance, in which case you would probably proceed with individualized counseling; but it may be only a particularly difficult phase of adolescence. In this case, you would probably meet with the parents and their son together, to provide family counseling.

The pattern of cannabis use by this adolescent is similar to that described in the medical report by Campbell et al.[15] At this writing it is not proven that heavy use of cannabis is causally linked to cerebral atrophy, but the counselor must be alerted to this possibility unless or until it is disproven.

In a case of behavioral deterioration associated with heavy use of cannabis every effort should be made to obtain a complete medical evaluation. If the condition is, in fact, associated with brain atrophy, it is likely that the patient would manifest some impairment in his ability to think, or to remember. He may have disturbances in sleep pattern and in speech, and he may be chronically nervous, irritable and jumpy. In the absence of drug use, such a pattern of behavior would justify referral to a specialist in neurology. In the presence of heavy use of cannabis, the appropriateness of neurological consultation or of major diagnostic studies such as pneumoencephalography must, in cases such as this, await the outcome of further attempts to validate the implications of Campbell *et al*. In any event, to assure follow-through in such a referral, care should be taken to avoid an atmosphere of alarm or panic about the possible outcome.

NOTES

1. See N. J. Doorenbos *et al.,* "Cultivation, Extraction and Analysis of *Cannabis sativa* L.," in *Marijuana: Chemistry, Pharmacology and Patterns of Social Usage,* Annals of the New York Academy of Sciences 191 (1971), 3–14.

2. *Ibid.*

3. F. T. Melges *et al.,* "Marihuana and Temporal Disintegration," *Science* 168 (29 May 1970): 1119.

4. J. H. Jaffe, "Drug Addiction and Drug Abuse," in *The Pharmacological Basis of Therapeutics,* 4th edition, ed. L. S. Goodman and A. Gilman (New York: Macmillan Company, 1970), p. 300.

5. D. E. McMillan, W. L. Dewey, and L. S. Harris, "Characteristics of Tetrahydrocannabinol Tolerance," in *Marijuana: Chemistry, Pharmacology and Patterns of Social Usage,* 83–99.

6. *Ibid.*

7. See L. Lemberger *et al.,* "Delta-9-Tetrahydrocannabinol: Metabolism and Disposition in Long-Term Marijuana Smokers," *Science* 173 (2 July 1971): 72–74.

8. E. Marcovitz and H. J. Myers, "The Marihuana Addict in the Army," *War Medicine* (Chicago) 6 (1944), 382–96.

9. J. H. Jaffe, "Drug Addiction and Drug Abuse," p. 300.

10. N. Q. Brill, "The Marihuana Problem," *Annals of Internal Medicine* 73, no. 3 (September 1970): 457.

11. For a more detailed discussion, see A. T. Weil, "Adverse Reaction to Marihuana: Classification and Suggested Treatment," *New England Journal of Medicine* 282, no. 18 (30 April 1970): 997–1000.

12. H. Kolansky and W. T. Moore, "Effects of Marihuana on Adolescents and Young Adults," *Journal of the American Medical Association* 216, no. 3 (19 April 1971): 486–92.

161

13. A. M. G. Campbell *et al.*, "Cerebral Atrophy in Young Cannabis Smokers," *The Lancet* (December 4, 1971): 1219–24.

14. N. Q. Brill, "The Marihuana Problem," p. 459.

15. A. M. G. Campbell *et al.*, "Cerebral Atrophy in Young Cannabis Smokers."

Chapter 7

CAFFEINE AND NICOTINE

Caffeine, theophylline, and theobromine are called the methylxanthines. All three of these agents stimulate the central nervous system, are diuretics (increase the production of urine by the kidney), increase the rate and force of contraction of the heart, and relax smooth muscles in the bronchi and blood vessels. The various methylxanthines differ in the intensity of their effects on these systems, with caffeine being the most powerful CNS stimulant of the three and theophylline being the most powerful cardiac stimulant and diuretic.

Caffeine is used therapeutically as a stimulant in the treatment of poisoning by depressants and in combination with analgesics, such as aspirin, for the relief of headaches. The other methylxanthines are medically used as cardiac stimulants, diuretics, and relaxants of the bronchial smooth muscle in the treatment of asthma. But by far the most common use of the methylxanthines is their consumption in common beverages.

The most popular methylxanthine beverages are coffee, tea, cocoa, and cola-flavored soft drinks. Both coffee and tea contain predominantly caffeine, from 100 mg to 150 mg per cup, which is the amount that is effective in reducing feelings of fatigue. Twelve ounces of a cola drink contain 35 mg to 55 mg of caffeine, and cocoa may contain up to 50 mg of

163

theobromine per cup. The degree to which an individual is stimulated by caffeine and the other methylxanthines varies. Some people can drink several cups of coffee in the evening and have no difficulty sleeping, but others may be unable to fall asleep for hours after a single cup of coffee.

The methylxanthines have a complex central nervous system pharmacology that is only just beginning to be unravelled. Surprisingly, however, in clinical medicine and psychiatry they often are not even considered to be drugs. But they *are* drugs, and their effects must be considered in combination with other drugs that are prescribed or taken non-medically. Because of the prevailing casual attitude toward methylxanthine effects, few questions have ever been asked about the effects of such drug combinations. Because of the same attitude, penetrating questions have never been asked about possible adverse effects of chronic use of methylxanthines by themselves or in combination with the many substances that are present in the plant sources of coffee and tea.

According to our definition of addiction (see Chapter 1) addiction to methylxanthines is rare, although some degree of psychological dependence may occur.[1] The term most applicable to patterns of methylxanthine use is habituation. This term is applied to a drug habit that requires some effort to break, but which is not at all associated with psychological or social impairment. Comparison with the effects of amphetamines suggests an explanation for the virtual absence of addiction to methylxanthines. While both drugs are anti-fatigue agents, the euphoria produced by methylxanthines is of lesser degree than that produced by amphetamines. Of added importance is the fact that beyond a certain dosage, methylxanthine effects are distinctly dysphoric: nervousness, jitteriness, and gastrointestinal symptoms occur. In contrast, euphoria is maintained or increased when amphetamine dosage is increased.

Nicotine is a natural alkaloid found in the leaves of the tobacco plant. Six hundred billion cigarettes are smoked annually in the United States.[2] Nicotine has no therapeutic use; rather, it is one of the most toxic of all drugs, acting with a rapidity comparable to that of cyanide. Nicotine can be absorbed not only from the gastrointestinal tract, but also through the skin and mucous membranes. The acutely fatal dose for a non-tolerant adult is probably 60 mg, although tolerance develops and the oral ingestion of approximately 2 grams has been survived.

The symptoms of a toxic dose of nicotine include nausea and salivation, abdominal pain, vomiting, diarrhea, cold sweat, headache, dizziness, confusion, disturbed hearing and vision, and marked weakness. Faintness and prostration ensue, and death results from respiratory failure due to paralysis of the muscles of respiration.

The smoke of an average cigarette may yield 6 mg to 8 mg of nicotine, and the smoke of a 10 gram cigar may yield 15 mg to 40 mg. Some nicotine in tobacco is burned during smoking, and the amount eventually absorbed depends upon many factors, including the moisture of the tobacco, the presence or absence of filters, the temperature of the smoke, and the frequency and depth of inhalation. Approximately 90 percent of the nicotine in inhaled smoke is absorbed, compared to 25 to 50 percent in the smoke that is drawn into the mouth and then expelled.[3]

Tobacco smoke also contains many other organic compounds, collectively known as tars, and significant amounts of carbon monoxide. Smoking cigarettes is associated with a higher incidence of lung cancer and emphysema (an obstructive lung disease). Furthermore, cigarette smokers have a higher death rate from heart disease and strokes than do non-smokers.[4] It is not known how much of this is due to the chronic pharmacological effect of nicotine and how much depends on other, perhaps unknown, factors.

While nicotine does have some effects on the central nervous system, in the usual doses the peripheral nervous system is most strikingly affected, especially the sympathetic nerves which contain hormones known as catecholamines. Secretion of catecholamines in sympathetic nerves and in the adrenal gland is altered by nicotine.[5] These effects are in part responsible for the effect of smoking on nervousness, either to increase it or decrease it.

A degree of physical dependence and some withdrawal symptoms may occur in cigarette smokers but addiction (see Chapter 1) is rare, i.e., in spite of even heavy smoking the user remains relatively unimpaired psychologically and behaviorally. With regard to smoking we therefore speak of habituation; as with caffeine, increasing the dose of nicotine beyond a certain point may produce the manifestations of poisoning which are markedly dysphoric.

QUESTIONS

1. Caffeine can be a poison.

                              True or false? . . . . . .

2. Caffeine is contraindicated in people suffering from peptic ulcer.

                              True or false? . . . . . .

3. Psychological dependence occurs with caffeine.

                              True or false? . . . . . .

4. Caffeine causes chromosome breakage.

                              True or false? . . . . . .

5. Stopping cigarette smoking lessens the likelihood of lung cancer.

                              True or false? . . . . . .

6. Nicotine is a tranquilizer.

                              True or false? . . . . . .

ANSWERS

1. Caffeine can be a poison.

Answer: *True*. In animals, an overdose of caffeine produces convulsions and death from respiratory failure. In man, the fatal oral dose is estimated to be 10 grams, the amount contained in sixty to a hundred cups of coffee. Unpleasant reactions may be observed after ingestion of one gram or more of caffeine. These may include insomnia, restlessness, excitement, sensory disturbances, tremulousness, diuresis, and heart palpitations.

2. Caffeine is contraindicated in people suffering from peptic ulcer.

Answer: *True*. Caffeine stimulates the gastric secretion of acid, most markedly in those persons who have a predisposition to the development of ulcers. A person with an active peptic ulcer should eliminate or restrict his intake of caffeinated beverages.

3. Psychological dependence occurs with caffeine.

Answer: *True*. Some degree of tolerance and psychological dependence may be associated with the methylxanthine beverages. But the "coffee break" is such a common part of our culture that it is rarely acknowledged as being a drug habit. There is no positive evidence that consumption of these beverages is in any way harmful to the vast majority of people. On the other hand, the possibility of adverse effects of chronic use such as shortened life span or promotion of various illnesses has never been scientifically investigated in man. The feeling of well-being and increased performance afforded by a cup of coffee, although possibly obtained at the expense of a later decrease in performance, are experiences few individuals would care to give up.

4. Caffeine causes chromosome breakage.

Answer: *True*. Caffeine induces chromosome breakage in many organisms, including man.[6] The interpretation of this effect and evaluation of possible hazards remains to be determined by future research.

5. Stopping cigarette smoking lessens the likelihood of lung cancer.

Answer: *True*. Persons who have not smoked cigarettes for at least one year have a markedly reduced incidence of lung cancer. Furthermore, their incidences of heart disease and stroke are almost the same as those of the non-smoking population.[7]

6. Nicotine is a tranquilizer.

Answer: *False*. Nicotine is primarily a stimulating agent, although many people say they smoke because it calms their nerves. Habituated cigarette smokers, however, definitely display signs of anxiety and tension when deprived of cigarettes.

CASE 7-1

A thirty-two year-old physician is seen by his physician for a check-up. The physician-patient has been in good health and offers no complaints, but after his examination he describes to his examiner an interesting "experiment" that he conducted on himself recently.

The physician-patient says he first started drinking coffee eight years ago when he was an intern, as he felt it helped him maintain alertness during night duty. Since then he has drunk an average of three or four cups per day. About six months ago he began to notice a feeling of jitteriness during the day and an occasional inability to fall asleep at night. At first he was worried about his psychiatric condition, then wondered if he might have developed "coffee nerves." Two months ago he began drinking decaffeinated coffee exclusively and all these symptoms ceased. He is now convinced that caffeine was actually the cause of his symptoms, but says his wife scoffs and says it must all be in his head.

As the doctor's doctor how would you interpret this history?

(A) The wife was right.
(B) He should have seen a psychiatrist.
(C) This really was a case of "coffee nerves."

DISCUSSION

The wife's explanation (A) is a typical reaction of disbelief of the drug effect of caffeine on the part of those individuals who can drink methylxanthine beverages, often in large amounts, without suffering any apparent adverse effect. The psychiatric interpretation (B) is likewise incorrect. But if this was a case of "coffee nerves" (C) why would it have occurred at this particular time?

For as yet unknown reasons the behavioral reactions to caffeine not only display individual differences, but also differ in relation to the life cycle. It is not unusual, as in this case, for adverse reactions to caffeine to make their first appearance during the 30's or 40's. In the aged large doses of caffeine may, paradoxically, have a sedative effect.[8]

CASE 7-2

A forty-three year-old man comes to your office for a check-up. He is a salesman and has a high-pressure job. He is obese and reports that he is a chainsmoker and has been smoking between two and three packs a day for twenty-two years. He says that smoking helps him keep calm, that he has tried to quit several times, but that he couldn't last more than a day or two.

Physical examination reveals marked obesity and hypertension (high blood pressure).

In this situation, what would you do?

Suggest your own solution.

. . . .

. . . .

. . . .

. . . .

. . . .

DISCUSSION

This man is a prime candidate for a heart attack or a stroke. Cigarette smoking, obesity, and high blood pressure are all associated with increased incidence of cardiovascular and cerebrovascular disease. Over the past several years, this has become more or less common knowledge; yet this man, like many others, continues to smoke cigarettes and to remain overweight.

This case is perhaps a perfect summary of what we have talked about until now. There is no such thing as an isolated drug problem. Whenever you attempt to treat a person with a "drug problem," you must deal adequately with three factors in order to have even a small chance of success.

First, you must deal with the physical effects of the drug use. These may include malnutrition, cirrhosis of the liver, toxic psychoses, or a host of other effects, Second, you must attempt to deal with the psychological problems that are a result of the drug use. Both of these factors can be dealt with only when the person is in a more or less drug-free state. This usually means detoxification and withdrawal, or perhaps methadone maintenance in some cases of narcotic addiction. It is very difficult, if not futile, to attempt to treat the physical and psychological effects of a pattern of *compulsive* drug use without breaking this pattern and at least temporarily eliminating the drug, and its effects, from the patient's system.

But this is only part of the problem. The third and most important factor in the treatment of a person with a drug problem involves dealing with the personal and psychological problems that may have led him to the use of the drug in the first place. It is much easier to withdraw a narcotic addict and perhaps find him a job, than it is to deal adequately with those

173

pressures and problems, including the general environment, that may have made use of narcotics a desirable alternative. But any lasting success depends in large part upon the drug user's adaptation to a new life style, and this is most difficult to achieve.

Another thread that runs through the whole spectrum of people with drug problems is that you cannot help those who do not want to be helped. You may detoxify them or withdraw them, and you may even partially rehabilitate them, but unless they have a strong personal commitment to their own rehabilitation, they will most likely relapse into their former patterns of behavior.

This brings us back to the problem of what to tell this forty-three year-old man who smokes and eats too much. In many ways, cigarette smoking does resemble addiction. The significant difference is that the acute and short-term effects of the drug use do not seem to be very harmful to the person or to society. A man who has smoked a pack of cigarettes is not as dangerous to himself or to society as is the man who has consumed a bottle of whiskey, taken amphetamines, and so on. He does not have to commit crimes to raise the money to buy cigarettes. But in other ways, especially in the matter of psychological dependence and compulsive use, he closely resembles other people with drug problems.

You should tell him what you know about the relationship between cigarette smoking, obesity, high blood pressure, and various diseases; that it is your opinion he should stop smoking and lose weight; and that you will help him in any way you can. The rest is obviously up to him. You may not be able to do anything for this man because he does not want to change his behavior. You should appreciate by now how complex and difficult a situation like this can be. You can rarely solve people's problems for them. You can more often help them solve their own problems themselves.

NOTES

1. J. Murdoch Ritchie, "The Xanthines," in *The Pharmacological Basis of Therapeutics,* 4th edition, ed. L. S. Goodman and A. Gilman (New York: Macmillan Company, 1970), p. 368.

2. R. L. Volle and G. B. Koelle, "Ganglionic Stimulating and Blocking Agents," in *The Pharmacological Basis of Therapeutics,* 4th edition, p. 590.

3. *Ibid.*

4. U. S. Department of Health, Education, and Welfare, *The Health Consequences of Smoking: 1969 Supplement to the 1967 Public Health Service Review* (Washington: U.S. Government Printing Office, 1969), pp. 3–5.

5. Volle and Koelle, "Ganglionic Stimulating and Blocking Agents."

6. P. S. Moorehead *et al.,* "Cytogenetic Methods for Mutagenicity Testing" in *Drugs of Abuse: Their Genetic and Other Chronic Nonpsychiatric Hazards,* ed. S. S. Epstein (Cambridge, Mass.: M.I.T. Press, 1971) p. 165.

7. U. S. Department of Health, Education, and Welfare, *The Health Consequences of Smoking,* p. 55.

8. Dr. Frank M. Barry has repeatedly observed the sedative effect of caffeine-sodium benzoate injection in post-operatively excited or psychotic elderly patients. Except for this special situation the injection of this drug causes hyperactivity and excitement.

BIBLIOGRAPHICAL ESSAY

The single best source of pharmacological information concerning the drugs discussed in this book is *The Pharmacological Basis of Therapeutics,* edited by Louis S. Goodman and Alfred Gilman. The text, which is known among medical students as the "blue bible," contains accurate, thorough, descriptive material and comprehensive reference lists. The fourth edition was published in New York by the Macmillan Company in 1970.

Jerome H. Jaffe, "Drug Addiction and Drug Abuse," on pages 276–313 of this book, is recommended especially for further study. Jaffe considers the following drugs: narcotic analgesics, alcohol, hypnotics, tranquilizers, amphetamines, cocaine, hallucinogens, and marihuana. He summarizes the chief features of each group of drugs and discusses such general topics as the etiology, treatment, and prevention of drug abuse.

NARCOTIC ANALGESICS

Jaffe deals specifically with the narcotic analgesics in Chapter 15, pages 237–75, in *The Pharmacological Basis of Therapeutics*. The pharmacological properties and therapeutic uses of all of the narcotic analgesics and narcotic antagonists are presented in detail, and Jaffe includes enough information to answer nearly all the questions about the narcotics that can at present be answered.

The following two articles describe the medical complications of narcotic addiction: Donald B. Louria, Terry Hensle, and John Rose, "The Major Medical Complications of Heroin Addiction," *Annals of Internal Medicine* 67, no. 1 (July 1967): 1–22, and Charles E. Cherubin, "The Medical Sequelae of Narcotic Addiction," *Annals of Internal Medicine* 67, no. 1 (July 1967): 23–33. The Louria, Hensle, Rose article presents cases seen by the authors, and both articles review the literature on the subject of narcotic addiction. Most of the information is specifically medical in orientation and quite detailed, but both articles can nevertheless be easily understood by the layman who is interested in the subject.

In "Successful Treatment of 750 Criminal Addicts," *Journal of the American Medical Association* 206, no. 12 (16 December 1968): 2708–11, the authors, Vincent P. Dole, Marie E. Nyswander, and Alan Warner, describe a four-year trial of methadone blockade for heroin addiction. The authors report a 94 percent success in ending the criminal activities of former addicts who underwent the methadone blockade treatment. The evaluation of this program is reported on by the Methadone Maintenance Evaluation Committee in "Progress Report of Evaluation of Methadone Maintenance Treatment Program as of March 31, 1968," which was a special communication published in the *Journal of the American Medical Association* 206, no. 12 (16 December 1968): 2712–14. In this report, the committee recommends continuation and expansion of the program, with continuing research and follow-up.

Marion K. Sanders examines, from a social and political viewpoint, the various theories of rehabilitation of heroin addicts and the proponents of the theories in "Addicts and Zealots," *Harper's Magazine,* June 1970, pages 71–80. Sanders describes each of the major programs and provides a rational explanation for the social complexities surrounding the problem of rehabilitation and treatment of heroin addicts.

In "Drugs without Crime," *Harper's Magazine,* July 1971, pages 60–72, Edgar May explains the British system of dealing with the problem of heroin addiction and compares the British situation to the situation in the United States. He outlines the advantages and disadvantages of the British system of dealing with heroin addiction and discusses the relevance of the British experience to problems in the United States with heroin addiction and crime.

Other references that were consulted on the subject of narcotics are Abraham Wikler *et al.,* "Effects of Frontal Lobotomy on the Morphine Abstinence Syndrome in Man: An Experimental Study," *AMA Archives of Neurology and Psychiatry* 67, no. 4 (April 1952): 510–21; and the *New York Times,* 23 September 1968, pages 1–34.

ALCOHOL

A very fine general reference on the subject of alcoholism is the *Manual on Alcoholism,* published by the American Medical Association in 1968. The nature of alcoholism, its diagnosis, and its treatment are examined, and the metabolism and pharmacology of alcohol are discussed. The manual is an excellent source of both detailed and general information on alcoholism.

J. Murdoch Ritchie outlines the pharmacological actions of alcohol on the various organ systems and physiologic functions of the body in "The Aliphatic Alcohols," pages 135–50, in *The Pharmacological Basis of Therapeutics.* Tolerance and addiction to alcohol and the therapeutic uses of alcohol are also discussed. The article is also of value for the author's list of references on this subject.

In the "Biological Concomitants of Alcoholism," *New England Journal of Medicine* 283, no. 1 (2 July 1970): 24–32, and no. 2 (9 July 1970): 71–81, Jack H. Mendelson supplies a thorough, detailed, and up-to-date review of all the physiological and medical complications of alcoholism. Mendelson provides 157 references that can be of additional value to the person interested in more information on the subject of alcoholism.

Other references cited in the text include Thomas A. Gonzales and Alexander O. Gettler, "Alcohol and the Pedestrian in Traffic Accidents," *Journal of the American Medical Association* 117, no. 18 (1 November 1941): 1523–25; David M. Spain, Victoria A. Bradess, and Andrew A. Eggston, "Alcohol and Violent Death: A One Year Study of Consecutive Cases in a Representative Community," *Journal of the American Medical Association* 146, no. 4 (26 May 1951): 334–35; and Richard L. Holcomb, "Alcohol in Relation to Traffic Accidents," *Journal of the American Medical Association* 111, no. 12 (17 September 1938): 1076–85.

HYPNOTICS AND TRANQUILIZERS

Of particular value on the subject of hypnotics and tranquilizers are two chapters in *The Pharmacological Basis of Therapeutics* by Seth K. Sharpless: "Hypnotics and Sedatives: The Barbiturates," pages 98–120, and "Hypnotics and Sedatives: Miscellaneous Agents," pages 121–34. Sharpless discusses the pharmacology of all of the hypnotics that are presently available. Another chapter in the same text, Murray E. Jarvik's "Drugs Used in the Treatment of Psychiatric Disorders," pages 151–203, outlines the pharmacology of and therapeutic uses for the major and minor tranquilizers. Jarvik also discusses the antidepressants, a group of drugs not generally abused, and the hallucinogens.

In his editorial, "Advertising and Abuse of Drugs," *New England Journal of Medicine* 284, no. 14 (8 April 1971): 789–90, Robert Seidenberg points out instances of inappropriate advertising of tranquilizers and questions the propriety of such advertising in medical journals. He calls for the adoption of standards for tranquilizer prescription and use.

Another reference cited in the text was Havelock F. Fraser *et al.*, "Degree of Physical Dependence Induced by Secobarbital or Phenobarbital." *Journal of the American Medical Association* 166, no. 2 (11 January 1958): 126–29.

AMPHETAMINES AND COCAINE

On the subject of amphetamines and cocaine, the following two chapters in *The Pharmacological Basis of Therapeutics* are of considerable significance: J. Murdoch Ritchie, Peter J. Cohen, and Robert D. Dripps, "Cocaine, Procaine and Other Synthetic Local Anesthetics," pages 371–401, and Ian R. Innes and Mark Nickerson, "Drug Acting on Postganglionic Adrenergic Nerve Endings and Structures Innervated by Theme (Sympathomimetic Drugs)," pages 478–523. The Ritchie, Cohen, Dripps chapter outlines the pharmacology and therapeutic uses of cocaine; the Innes-Nickerson chapter begins with a lesson in the functioning of the sympathetic branch of the autonomic nervous system and goes on to discuss the pharmacology and therapeutic uses of all the sympathomimetic drugs. Both chapters are of additional value for the extensive references that are provided.

Einar S. Perman's editorial, "Speed in Sweden," *New England Journal of Medicine* 283, no. 14 (1 October 1970): 760–61, describes the intravenous abuse of amphetamines as the most serious of all drug-abuse problems in Sweden. Perman presents the historical context of the problem as well as the steps that have been taken to combat the problem. A second editorial in the same journal, "And Pep in America," pages 761–62, examines the relevance of the Swedish experience to the growing problem of amphetamine abuse in the United States.

In "Amphetamine Abuse: Patterns and Effects of High Doses Taken Intravenously," *Journal of the American Medical Association* 201, no. 5 (31 July 1967): 89–93, the authors, John C. Kramer, Vitezslav S. Fischman, and Don C. Littlefield, vividly describe the behavior pattern of alternating "runs and crashes" associated with intravenous use of high doses of amphetamines. The authors also discuss the social and psychological concomitants of this behavior pattern and the acute and chronic effects of this type of amphetamine abuse.

B. Philip Citron *et al.,* "Necrotizing Angiitis Associated with Drug Abuse," *New England Journal of Medicine* 283, no. 19 (5 November 1970): 1003–11, is a study of the incidence of a disease called necrotizing angiitis in fourteen drug abusers. Four of the patients died, and postmortem information on their deaths is included in the article. Most of the patients reported on the study were multiple drug users, but the authors speculate that intravenous methamphetamine use is the common denominator in the etiology of this disease.

Another reference cited in the text was "Dependence on Amphetamines and Other Stimulant Drugs," a statement prepared by the AMA Committee on Alcoholism and Addiction and published in the *Journal of the American Medical Association* 197, no. 12 (19 September 1966): 1023–27.

HALLUCINOGENS

On the subject of hallucinogens, Murray E. Jarvik's "Drugs Used in the Treatment of Psychiatric Disorders," pages 151–

203, in *The Pharmacological Basis of Therapeutics* is helpful. In Part IV of his chapter, Jarvik discusses the pharmacology of mescaline and LSD. In his very comprehensive review "On the Use and Abuse of LSD," *Archives of General Psychiatry* 18 (March 1968): 330–47, Daniel X. Freedman discusses LSD use from a social and psychological perspective. Freedman describes the effects of LSD quite vividly, and also considers, at some length, the topics of motivations for use of the drug, psychiatric complications of LSD, and the risk of "bad trips."

In their article "LSD and Genetic Damage," *Science* 172, (30 April 1971): 431–40, Norman I. Dishotsky and his colleagues present their conclusions, based on a thorough review of all the major studies of LSD and genetic damage, that pure LSD ingested in moderate doses does not damage chromosomes *in vivo* (in living persons), does not cause detectable genetic damage, and is not a teratogen (a substance that produces birth defects) or a carcinogen (a substance that produces cancer) in man. Over ninety studies are reviewed, and a comprehensive list of references is provided by the authors. One of the studies reviewed in this article is Margaret J. Corey's "Chromosome Studies on Patients (In Vivo) and Cells (In Vitro) Treated with Lysergic Acid Diethylamide," *New England Journal of Medicine* 282, no .17 (23 April 1970): 939–43. The Corey study exemplifies the complex methodology that is required to undertake such chromosome studies.

Another study cited in the text was William H. McGlothlin, Robert H. Sparkes, and David O. Arnold, "Effects of LSD on Human Pregnancy," *Journal of the American Medical Association* 212, no. 9 (1 June 1970): 1483–87. The authors found no statistically significant data concerning any causal relationships between LSD use and spontaneous abortions, premature births, or birth defects.

The most comprehensive review of toxic effects of hallucinogens as well as all psychoactive drugs is *Drugs of Abuse: Their Genetic and Other Nonpsychiatric Hazards,* edited by Samuel S. Epstein (Cambridge, Mass.: M.I.T. Press, 1971).

The results of chemical determinations done on "street" drugs are reported by Frances E. Cheek, Stephens Newell, and Milton Joffe in "Deceptions in the Illicit Drug Market," *Science* 167 (27 February 1970): 1276.

MARIHUANA

The following four articles are of particular value on the subject of marihuana: Leo E. Hollister, "Marihuana in Man: Three Years Later," *Science* 172 (2 April 1971): 21–29; Richard C. Pillard, "Marihuana," *New England Journal of Medicine* 283, no. 6 (6 August 1970): 294–303; Carl M. Lieberman and Beth W. Lieberman, "Marihuana—A Medical Review," *New England Journal of Medicine* 284, no. 2 (14 January 1971): 88–91; and Norman Q. Brill *et al.,* "The Marihuana Problem," *Annals of Internal Medicine* 73, no. 3 (September 1970): 449–65. The Hollister article is the most comprehensive and up to date, and the Brill article presents detailed information on patterns of marihuana use. All of the articles are objective, easy to read, and well-documented. A fifth article, "Marihuana Chemistry," *Science* 178 (5 June 1970): 1159–66, is a comprehensive and detailed report by Raphael Mechoulam, one of the world's authorities on the subject of marihuana chemistry.

The first recent attempt to do a controlled experimental study of marihuana effects is reported by Andrew T. Weil, Norman E. Zinberg, and Judith M. Nelsen in "Clinical and Psychological Effects of Marihuana in Man," *Science* 162 (13 December 1968): 1234–42. The subjects of this study were given either marihuana or a placebo to smoke, and psychological and physiological tests were then performed to determine the effects of marihuana use on the subjects. In "Adverse Reactions to Marihuana: Classification and Suggested Treatment," *New England Journal of Medicine* 282, no. 18 (30 April 1970): 998–1000, Andrew T. Weil describes and classifies the most commonly seen adverse reactions to acute marihuana use. He also prescribes therapeutic strategies for these reactions. The paper is based on the author's experience in hospital practice in San Francisco, where he had the opportunity to treat many such persons who suffered adverse reactions.

A highly controversial article on the effects of marihuana use is Harold Kolansky and William T. Moore, "Effects of Marihuana on Adolescents and Young Adults," *Journal of the American Medical Association* 216, no. 3 (19 April 1971): 486–92. The authors report several instances of adverse psychological and behavioral changes due to chronic use of marihuana. They describe patients who demonstrated neurologic signs and symptoms, and patients who were psychotic. Many persons have taken issue with the validity of the authors' conclusions, but the report clearly indicates a need for further research in the actual association between chronic marihuana use and adverse psychological changes.

Other references cited in the text include: Frederick T. Melges, *et al.*, "Marihuana and Temporal Disintegration," Science 168 (29 May 1970): 1118–20; Jerome H. Jaffe, "Drug Addiction and Drug Abuse," in *The Pharmacological Basis of Therapeutics*, pages 276–313; Louis Lemberger *et al.*, "Marihuana: Studies on the Disposition and Metabolism of Delta-9-Tetrahydrocannabinol in Man," *Science* 170 (18 December 1970): 1320–22; Louis Lemberger *et al.*, "Delta-9-Tetrahydrocannabinol: Metabolism and Disposition in Long-Term Marihuana Smokers," *Science* 173 (2 July 1971): 72–73; D. E. McMillan, W. L. Dewey, and L. S.

Harris, "Characteristics of Tetrahydrocannabinol Tolerance," in *Marijuana: Chemistry, Pharmacology and Patterns of Social Usage,* Annals of the New York Academy of Sciences 191 (1971), 83–99.

Much of our most recently acquired knowledge of the botanical, chemical, and pharmacological aspects of marihuana has been summarized in the conference of May 20 and 21, 1971 of the New York Academy of Sciences, entitled: *Marijuana: Chemistry, Pharmacology and Patterns of Social Usage,* vol. 191 of the Annals of the New York Academy of Sciences.

Another excellent and concise review is the Report of a World Health Organization Scientific Group entitled "The Use of Cannabis," in *World Health Organization Technical Report Series* No. 478, Geneva, 1971.

A most important, if alarming, recent report on a possible serious complication of chronic heavy use of cannabis is that of A. M. G. Campbell, *et al.,* "Cerebral Atrophy in Young Cannabis Smokers," *The Lancet* (December 4, 1971): 1219–24. The same issue contains an editorial (p. 1240) about the problem of finding appropriate controls for the cerebral-atrophy patients. The editorial emphasizes our current lack of knowledge about gross brain defects in behavior disorders in general, whether associated with drug abuse or not.

CAFFEINE AND NICOTINE

J. Murdoch Ritchie discusses the pharmacology, history, therapeutic uses, and nonmedical uses of caffeine, theophylline, and theobromine in his "Central Nervous System Stimulants: The Xanthines," pages 358–70, in *The Pharmacological Basis of Therapeutics.* Ritchie's article is also of value for the additional references he gives on this subject.

The history and pharmacology of nicotine are presented and discussed, particularly in relation to the neurophysiology of the autonomic nervous system, by Robert L. Volle and George B. Koelle in "Ganglionic Stimulating and Blocking Agents," pages 585–600, in *The Pharmacological Basis of Therapeutics*. Another publication of value on this subject is the report of the U.S. Department of Health, Education, and Welfare, *The Health Consequences of Smoking: 1969 Supplement to the 1967 Public Health Service Review* (Washington: U.S. Government Printing Office, 1969). This report summarizes the current knowledge of the relationships between smoking and heart disease, strokes, chronic obstructive lung disease (chronic bronchitis and emphysema), cancer, and noncancerous oral disease.

INDEX

Addiction, definition of, 4

Alcohol, 35–60; absorption of, 36; acute physiological effects of, 36; blood concentrations of, achieved by ingestion, 45–46; cross tolerance with general depressants, 43; effects of, on sexual function, 47; feelings of warmth caused by, 46; legal determination of intoxication from, 45–46; medical complication of consumption of, 37; metabolism of, 36–37, 46; overdose of, in combination with sleeping pills, 45, (*see also* Hypnotics); patterns of use of, 35; tolerance to the effects of, 36–37; relation of, to traffic accidents, 35, 46; value of, as a nutrient, 45; withdrawal syndromes associated with, 37–38

Alcoholic personality. *See* Alcoholism, psychological factors in

Alcoholics Anonymous, 38–39 (in cases, 50, 54). *See also* Alcoholism, treatment of

Alcoholism: definition of, 35–36; denial and rationalization associated with, 39–40; effects of, on life expectancy, 44; psychological factors in, 38,

46–47; suspicion of (case), 48–51; treatment of, 38–40, 44, 59

Amphetamine (Benzedrine, Dexedrine), 88. *See also* Amphetamines

Amphetamines, 88–116; associated with violent behavior, 95; chief causes of death among addicts, 97; combined use of, with depressants, 95 (case, 112–15); compared with cocaine, 91, 96; compulsive abuse, oral (case), 106–8; compulsive abuse, intravenous (case), 109–11; effects of, on paradoxical sleep, 89; intermittent use of (case), 98–101; medical uses of, 89; patterns of use and abuse of, 88-90; psychological effects of, 88; "rush" produced by intravenous use of, 96–97; tolerance to the effects of, 89, 90, 96; toxic effects of, 90–91; use of, by athletes, 94; withdrawal from, 90

Analgesic, definition of, 5

Ascites, definition of, 52

Barbiturates, 61–64, 68–77; addiction to, 63; chief uses of, 61–62; as anticonvulsant, 62;

Methylxanthines, 163–64; compared with amphetamines, 164; dependance on, 164
Methyprylon (Noludar), 61. See also Hypnotics
Miltown. See Meprobamate
Minimal brain dysfunction, 89
Minor tranquilizers, 64–65, 71–72, 81–86, 112–15; combined use of, with amphetamines (case), 112–15; effects of, on feelings of anxiety, 71–72; patterns of abuse of, 65 (case, 81–86); role of, in the therapy of emotional difficulties, 64–65, 71–72 (case, 81–86); tolerance to, 65, 83; toxic reactions to, 83–84; withdrawal from, 65
Miosis, definition of, 5–6
Morphine, 5. See also Narcotic analgesics
Mydriasis, definition of, 88

Narcolepsy, 89
Narcotic analgesics, 3–34; addiction to, 6; addiction to, propensity of individuals for, 14–15; addiction to, role of pusher in, 14; causes of death from use of, 15, 16; dangers of self-administration of, 18; description of properties of, 5–7; differences in abuse potential of, 17; dysphoria as a response to, 14; effects of, on drives, 15; legal indications for medical use of, 8; physical dependence on, in the newborn, 14; withdrawal syndrome, 6–7; withdrawal syndrome, danger of fatality from, 16. See also Heroin; Methadone maintenance
Narcotic antagonists, 10
Narcotic antagonist maintenance, 10
Native American Church, 118
Necrotizing angiitis, 97
Needle fixation (case), 31–33
Nembutal. See Pentobarbital
Nicotine, 165–66, 169, 172–75. amount of, absorbed during smoking, 165; calming effects of, reported, 169; chronic use of (case), 172–74; effects of, on nervous system, 166; habituation to, 166; patterns of use of, 165; toxicity of, 165. See also Cigarette smoking
Nitrous oxide, 69
Norepinephrine, 96, 117
Nutritional amblyopia, 37

Odyssey House. See Therapeutic community

Pain, 6
Pancreatitis, 37
Paraldehyde, 61 See also Hypnotics
Pellagra, 37
Pentobarbital (Nembutal), 63. See also Hypnotics
Peripheral neuropathies, 37
Phenobarbital, 62. See also Hypnotics
Phenothiazines. See Major tranquilizers
Phoenix House. See Therapeutic

This book was set in eleven point Times Roman. It was composed, printed and bound by Benson Printing Company, Nashville, Tennessee. The paper is Jackson Offset 60 pound, manufactured by Allied Paper Incorporated. The design is by LaWanda J. McDuffie.